Dancers Amongst The Stars

The wonder, the beauty and the magic of who we really are, seen through the eyes of an awakening woman, who happens to have a therapist in her pocket

JANNY JUDDLY,

'The Therapist in my Pocket'

BALBOA.
PRESS
A DIVISION OF HAY HOUSE

Balboa Press books may be ordered through booksellers or by contacting:

Balboa Press
A Division of Hay House
1663 Liberty Drive
Bloomington, IN 47403
www.balboapress.com
1 (877) 407-4847

Because of the dynamic nature of the Internet, any web addresses or links contained in this book may have changed since publication and may no longer be valid. The views expressed in this work are solely those of the author and do not necessarily reflect the views of the publisher, and the publisher hereby disclaims any responsibility for them.

The author of this book does not dispense medical advice or prescribe the use of any technique as a form of treatment for physical, emotional, or medical problems without the advice of a physician, either directly or indirectly. The intent of the author is only to offer information of a general nature to help you in your quest for emotional and spiritual well-being. In the event you use any of the information in this book for yourself, which is your constitutional right, the author and the publisher assume no responsibility for your actions.

Any people depicted in stock imagery provided by Thinkstock are models, and such images are being used for illustrative purposes only.
Certain stock imagery © Thinkstock.

Printed in the United States of America.

ISBN: 978-1-4525-9936-6 (sc)
ISBN: 978-1-4525-9938-0 (hc)
ISBN: 978-1-4525-9937-3 (e)

Library of Congress Control Number: 2014920859

Balboa Press rev. date: 12/04/2014

Contents

. . . .

Acknowledgments

· ·

This is a very special and magical book; in fact, it is unique. The words are mine, but the energy contained within it is that of so many wonderful friends, their laughter, their wisdom, their belief and insight, their fun and sheer exuberance. I recognize them as my soul tribe.

And so, rather than producing some kind of dry list of acknowledgments, I wanted to convey, in the best way I could think of, a flavor of the wonderful people, all over the world, whom I am honored to call friends. It is they who have helped me to see what I had, convinced me that I should share it, and have showed me over and over again that what I was writing was worthy of a book.

It is to these wonderful people, therefore, that I acknowledge my enormous appreciation and gratitude. Here are some of their amazing voices. They speak for themselves. Love and sparkles!

DIANNE HALL-ROCKWELL (MASSACHUSETTS)

Books have always been portals for me, and the authors that move me the most are the noticers, the listeners, and feelers, for they write of the little things that make us human. They *know* us, and the seemingly insignificant happenings that rock our world and change us forever. They comfort and identify with our hurting five year old, lonely teenager, excited, nervous new parent, and grieving adult. They *are* us. They bring up to the surface the magic of childhood play and imagination, and help us to rediscover that joy through their words, remind us who we are and why we came, and fan the flame that we all carry.

I am so blessed to include Janny in my favorite authors list, for she is such a dear rememberer, and acknowledger of all of our little pieces. And did I mention sparkles? She invented them, a long, long time ago. You have so touched my life, kiddo- and it is great walking this path with you again. No one in the world deserves this recognition more than you... and I could not be happier if it was me. Wait... you *are* me! And I am full to over-flowing with love and joy for you.

EILEEN BRADISH (NEW YORK)

Janny, your writings move me deeply. You have the incredible gift of being able to put into words those emotions many of us find indescribable. Each line that I read brings me closer to an understanding of which my soul has always known, but my mind had forgotten. Thank you for sharing your gift with us. Your words will be forever treasured.

DEBRA MITTLER (CALIFORNIA)

Janny, you are truly a Beautiful Angel whose profound wisdom and loving energy speaks right to my heart and soul. You are truly a blessing, Love, and I am so glad you are sharing your voice, the spirit of *love* and *wisdom* in the world. I am so grateful to you and for you, you are one of the reasons Facebook has become a great adventure. Wishing, or might I say, knowing your book is going to be, a *huge* success and I cannot wait to purchase it. Loving you my friend!

ELIZABETH WARD (SURREY, UK)

Janny is an undimmable light.......her radiance and love is a gift to us all and her wise words are a precious and unquenchable source of comfort and joy to me and, I suspect, many others!

KASTURI MUKHERJEE (MAHARASHTRA)

Sometimes in life's journey, we get to know and love people who we may never see or meet in person. Janny, through her soul and her words, has reached out and touched me, healed me, made me laugh, cry, ponder on things that were once beyond my understanding, and sometimes has simply reached out through time and space and given me a giant big hug. And then, there is the magical love and sparkles that she quite literally adds from her very heart, to everything she writes.

SHIHAAM PECK (CAPE TOWN)

Dear Janny, as a woman, especially at this time of change and unfolding, you are the epitome of the Goddess energy of our New Earth. You share, you do not teach/preach. You walk alongside us holding a space that says, 'I'm with you. I got your back. You are safe'. When I needed guidance, you empowered me, and at those times when I was ready to heal, it was right there on my news feed in a story that felt like you had just weaved a quilt in all my colors and textures. I was drawn into the story so deeply that some really moved me to painful tears. What more divine timing could there be. You have, or soon will have, revolutionized the way the world looks at therapy. Thank you for being so authentic, selfless, yet so true to yourself. You have helped me be authentically me. Blessings always!

DAFFANIE SANDERS (TEXAS)

You are amazing and to be able to witness your journey is beyond words. Thank you for being the miraculous mirror that you are!

CARL CHASE (CALIFORNIA)

My dear friend Janny Juddly is one of the most insightful people I have ever had the pleasure of reading. She has the knack of putting her insights within a story, which cleverly bypasses the critical factor within us, so the truth of her messages can be realized with an open mind. I am so very excited to know she is publishing her works so that everyone can have access to this amazing collection of insights.

AL NICH (FLORIDA)

Your life exudes brilliance, like no other, you are that light that shines softly and forever. You give life to so many near and far. I know the words that come alive in this book will be a blessing to all that read it.

DIANE KOROL (BRITISH COLUMBIA)

Janny, I am delighted to offer you my words of love and support. My desire is that my words reach you wrapped in all the love and gratitude with which they are offered. Your words and your presence are a daily delight and inspiration in my life. You share loving wisdom in a way that is enchanting and delightful. Your writing sparkles and shimmers in the heart and soul as it enlightens, uplifts, inspires and delights you.

DONNA ARMSTRONG (BRITISH COLUMBIA, CANADA)

Light brought to the soul in such honoring loving kindness...awaken with Janny. Your gift awaits!

JONI ABBATECOLA (NEW JERSEY)

When my two very dear friends died, I joined the groups Janny is in online. They saved my life. Janny's constant kind and insightful presence kept me going. I needed her expertise as a therapist and a spiritual being. Being a therapist myself, I am fussy! However, her posts were so genuine, compassionate, and heartfelt; my heart was able to respond. I would not have stayed with the group initially except for her prolific writings. I cannot thank her enough.

HARIATA HAMA (NEW ZEALAND)

Therapist Janny Juddly shares deep wisdom and profundity - with sparkles! Always encouraging and down-to -Earth, you will find her inspirations relevant and uplifting. Very highly recommended.

DARLENE GAIL JUBERT (NEW YORK)

The Universe knew I needed someone to help me through the loss of my life partner after twenty-nine wonderful years. So it conspired that Janny and I should meet virtually since we are an ocean apart from two different countries. Janny's words were sometimes in direct response to mine or were those she was inspired to share with all but either way her heartfelt and insightful words came just when I needed them most. For that, I am forever grateful and blessed. Thank you Janny! You are truly an inspiration!

TERESA MITCHEL (KENTUCKY)

Sharing ideas with Janny brings Sparkles that brighten the grey of Gloom until it exists No More!

CANDACE O'CONNOR (U.S)

Janny Juddly, aka The Therapist in My Pocket, is an amazing woman and a dear friend, even though I know her only through the miles. I am eagerly awaiting her book! The unfolding of this journey has been extraordinary and one that I am honored, as a member of her soul family, to have shared. She has consistently helped and guided me in my own spiritual growth. It is a true joy to call her my friend!

JESSIE D ANDERSON (ILLINOIS)

You have an inner peace about you that eludes many and I know, for myself, that is what I would like to achieve as well.

MONALISA LOBATO (SPAIN)

In life, there comes a moment when people are placed on our path, to open our minds, our hearts. And not until then, do we realize why. I am sitting here with tears in my eyes. Hey...if we can inspire one person a day to be better and happier... life becomes a breeze....

CAROLIN POST (CALGARY, CANADA)

Janny has been medicine for my soul. She helps cultivate our true selves. Her words melt perfectly like chocolate chips in warm cookies, bringing comfort, and clarity.

YZZIE V ATSITAUB (PHILIPPINES)

My journey is like a walk on a lavender field with you Miss Janny... magical!

I feel our being brought together has been by Divine intention...I am just expressing my thoughts as I read your posts, every day.

They have lifted me up, held my hand, given me a gentle push, nudge. And your smile always lingers if am not in front of the computer. Honestly, I have kept your posts on my mobile phone, and if I do not have any internet connection around, I just linger over your posts I saved here.

It's like you are my fairy goddess of love and sparkles...there is always this deep sense of gratitude I feel for you and a warmth within my chest whenever you inspire me...bless you more Miss Janny! Love to you!

JEN HELVIE (MICHIGAN)

Janny Juddly writes words that will touch your soul and make you realize you are never alone.

BARBARA MORGAN (LEICESTERSHIRE, UK)

It has been such a privilege to watch the unfolding of The Therapist in My Pocket. Janny has a deep understanding of the human psyche and of things Spiritual. She is able to put that knowledge into words in such a way that they reach into the heart of the reader with the result that they recognize themselves and feel known, perhaps for the very first time.

Dedication

· ·

There is one person, above all others, who has ensured that this book came to fruition. This amazing person has been with me through some of the darkest and some of the brightest and most sparkly moments of my life, is my rock and my comfort, can go wherever I go and stay in those places with me, knows, understands, and loves me with a tenderness and fierce loyalty beyond anything I have ever known.

They will talk excitedly and inspiringly with me for hours as we grow ideas. They will go for a walk or share crackers and cheese and cuppa after cuppa in the middle of the night. They reassure and ground me, convince me again and again that this was meant to be. Without this person's constant belief and trust in me, this book would not be here.

That person is my wonderful partner, soul mate, and best friend. Nicky, I owe you more, and love you more, than I can ever say. Thank you so much for showing up!

Foreword

Janny weaves her insights as a psychotherapist, her wisdom, inner knowing, and life experiences, gently into the most magical stories in her book "Dancers Amongst the Stars", stories that more often than not ignite a childhood memory within the adults who read them. They are always so refreshing, gentle, and soothing, like that gentle breeze that holds you in its warm embrace on a summer evening. She writes in a way that lays no blame or judgment on anyone, but rather leads the reader along a path to self-discovery. For me personally, some of Janny's stories gave me those huge amazing *aha* moments of such clarity, and recognition as to where some of my conditioning and beliefs had come from. Beliefs that did not serve me and which, once I saw them, I could set about changing, whilst other stories and verse were simply a joy to read and snuggle into.

For adults reading them, they lead you along a path to moments of such profound clarity, as you see where and how you created belief systems that may not serve the perfection of who you truly are. Belief systems that were just as often built on the loving solid foundations of a parent's misguided love and adoration as those that were built on foundations of rejection or lack of love.

They hold such empowering messages for children and adults alike. I see Janny's work as a powerful self-help tool, one that parents would love to have when guiding the wondrous children in their care into the future adult they will become. A book where the stories have children asking for more and parents happy to read, where both the child and the parent benefit from the story within. This is a book where there is going to be at the very least that one story that will touch a chord for the reader and help launch them on the path to self- discovery, self-empowerment and self-worth.

I have had the honor and pleasure to be there at the beginning as Janny started to share her stories and verse with us. As one who has read since I was a young child I knew in an instant that there was something powerful in her writing, writing that could reach everyone in a way that brought about the healing and self-empowerment that so many seek. Janny captures the reader and holds them gently as she takes them on a journey, for some it will be a journey of self-discovery and for others who may have already reached that place of inner peace it will be a journey none the less.

To Janny, I thank you for allowing me to be a part of this wondrous journey with you thus far, and I know for certain that this is just the first of many books you have within you that will light up the world of those that read them, and I look forward with a joyful glee to the unfolding of it all.

The following poem is dedicated to you!

Love you heaps my beautiful Soul Sister:

Reflections of Appreciation

As dawn ushered in a brand new day
The Sun found and kissed her face.
The room where she lay, lit up all around
Filled with her beauty and her grace

Today marked a special milestone.
For her this was quite unlike any other
She lay pondering her life thus far
As a daughter, sister, friend and mother

She reflected on the many moments
Strewn throughout this her earthly life
Most of these she had welcomed
Whilst some brought much angst and strife

With the knowledge and the wisdom
That only comes with passing years
She relished each moment for its gift
Her eyes shimmered, filled with tears

She embraced completely all the contrast
That life to her *now* in time had brought
She accepted ownership for the whole of it
Appreciation for all that she'd been taught.

She saw how all the paths that she had walked
In her varied earthly feminine roles
Now fed her heartfelt passion to talk the talk
That today inspired oh so many souls.

Today was a milestone, her sixtieth birthday
Some it would cause to shudder with fear
Thinking that as life passes much too quickly
Death for them must surely grow ever near

For her it brought much joy and peace
It touched her soul, with that inner knowing
For which she was eternally appreciative
The love in her heart now set to overflowing

For me, I am honoured to call this goddess friend
To share my journey beside her and see what unfolds
I'll embrace every day with her for as long as we have
And give daily appreciation for all that life holds.

© **Eileen Greaney**
2014
(Melbourne, Australia)

Introduction

· ·

It has been a strange and exciting time, these past two years, and in particular these past few months. I would like to tell you a little about it briefly, if I may. It will provide a little background to this book and how it came about.

I have been a psychotherapist in a thriving full time private practice, offering therapy and mindfulness and meditation, together with, more recently, spiritual mentoring and energy work, for over twenty five years. It is work I absolutely love. I had thought that this was what I would be doing for the rest of my working life.

However, two years ago, my life changed dramatically. My partner, Nicky, and I had gone away for the weekend, to an old cottage at the top of a steep hill in a Derbyshire village, one snowy weekend, and what happened there, and subsequently, turned my life on its head.

The roads were so bad, we wondered several times whether we were being foolhardy to even set out. However, Nicky had been convinced that, in some way, this cottage, and this weekend, were significant. That we were meant to come here. Nicky's intuition is always to be trusted, and so we set out, despite the appalling conditions.

We skidded and crawled at a snail's pace along the treacherous, but almost deserted, roads, for about two hours, and finally arrived, having to leave the car at the bottom of the tiny lane the cottage was on, and carry our bags, slipping and sliding, up to the top. Inside, we lit the log burner, popped the kettle on, and gradually dried out and warmed through. Then got ready for bed. We were tired after the journey and from carrying the bags, slipping and sliding, all the way up the hill in the snow. We just needed to sleep.

However, sleep was the last thing we were going to be doing.

As we lay in bed, the energy in the room began rising higher and higher. I can best describe it as an energy of immense joy. There was something utterly compelling about whatever it was that was happening. The energy was tangible, as in you could feel it pulsing through your body, as heat and tingling, and as an enormous surge of love and overwhelming happiness. I became aware that I was grinning and grinning uncontrollably. In fact, I could not stop grinning; the energy was so powerful.

Then, suddenly, something quite alarming began to happen. Streaks and balls of light started flashing across the room. More and more, and with increasing frequency. We would suddenly become aware of one, somewhere high on the ceiling, or behind our heads, and then see it send a bright flash of light across the room.

At first, it was frightening, and we lay under the bedclothes wondering what was going to happen to us, afraid to move. We spoke in whispers to each other, confirming and checking out what each of us was seeing. We would whisper, 'did you see that …oh, and that, there….and again…...' Strangely, and almost as if in direct response to our fear, the flashing lights would stop. At the same time, the level of energy in the room would drop a little. It was reassuring, at least. It felt like whatever this was had no intention of harm.

During one such lull, I got out of bed, in some trepidation and with great care, and looked for anything that might be emitting such light, something electrical, maybe. It seemed the most logical explanation. However, I could not find anything. Everything was still and uneventful, and there was certainly no visible or detectable source for what was happening.

Nevertheless, as I returned to bed, and we relaxed a little, becoming more trusting that nothing harmful was happening or intended, the lights began to flash again. Huge, powerful streaks of light, sometimes pure white light, sometimes with a hint of blue. In addition, as they did so, the energy of immense joy and love in the room became tangible once again.

This time, it went on for a good half an hour or more, and then slowly subsided, until all that was left was a pale form over in the corner, tall and reaching from floor to ceiling, which just remained there, quite still, but whose loving energy we could feel powerfully. We fell asleep feeling strangely safe and held in its loving embrace, which seemed to surround us but also to fill us.

The following morning, we tried to make sense of what had happened. We both remarked on the amazing energy of joy and love that had been in the room. We could both still recall it clearly. The very air seemed magical and crackling with energy and light.

Life has never been the same again. It was as if we had somehow acquired an extra sense, a way of seeing and experiencing, a knowing, a connection, a remembering. It is so hard to find the right words, because it was somehow beyond words. It was felt, sensed, known deep in our being. The world was new, because we saw it differently.

It was like suddenly being given a pair of magic spectacles, through which a world of color and sparkle and love, immense joy and compassion, a completely new way of seeing, was being revealed.

Outside in the sunlight, we were shocked and then awed to notice that everywhere we looked we could see sparkles in the air, millions and millions, going right up into the sky, and whenever we moved we could see energy, like pale, sparkly mist, moving all around us. We could also hear strange tinkling noises in our ears, of very high frequency, almost like joyous laughter and bells all rolled into one. The world had gained a dimension we had been completely unaware of before.

That was the beginning. Nothing has ever felt 'normal' since. We found we were drawn to new spiritual teachings, new ways of understanding the world and the universe. Leading edge thinking: Dr. Wayne Dyer, Eckhart Tolle, Abraham-Hicks, Gregg Braden, Bruce Lipton, Anita Moorjani, amongst many others. I felt driven to join Facebook groups in which a very new and different spirituality was being understood and shared, and to interact in ways that would never have interested me before.

I have always been a private person, but suddenly I was reaching out to total strangers whose thinking was similar to mine. I began to find that I had lots to offer, lots to say.

My head often felt as if it was bursting; would feel as if it could actually burst wide open. I would spend nights sweating and wide-awake as I felt energy rushing and tingling through me. And in the darkness, as I would lay in bed, always, millions of sparkles would be twinkling. I could see that the air was dense with energy, and I could make out different densities in the room. I would feel my face tickle as if something had fluttered against it, and I could feel my hair being stroked. The same high energy, the kind that would make me grin and grin, was always present.

I would catch strange scents, and at times hear music. One time I could hear Gregorian chants, another organ music, another an entire orchestra playing. Sometimes it would be the tinkling of bells, sometimes a sort of whispering in my ear, like lots of voices all speaking at once, but I could never make out the words. I would walk into my therapy room and find a white feather on my chair, or get out of the car and find a white feather at my feet as I stepped out, or on the doormat, or on the window ledge. In fact, they were everywhere I went. I became aware that 'signs' were everywhere, but had no idea what sense to make of them.

Things continued to happen with increasing frequency. I saw glistening light everywhere, figures of light moving, was aware of sparkling presences nearby often, and always at night in the darkness. I knew that something hugely significant was happening, but had no idea what. I was sharing all these things with people in the spiritual groups I belonged to on Facebook, who were excited to see where they led.

Then something new happened. Nicky and I started to see strings of light, and to hear the whisper of words we could not quite make out. We puzzled over what all this could possibly mean. We even wondered if we were imagining things or going crazy. However, one day, it was more than whispers. The voices were clearer, and what they whispered contained something very new. They spoke excitedly, and with a certain authority. They said it like it was the most natural thing to say, almost self-evident. They said it as if we would know what they meant. They said, quite urgently, "Hurry up; we've got a book to write."

Shortly afterwards, I began to feel drawn to write. It was very specific writing, drawing on both my numerous years of psychotherapy experience and the new thinking about spirituality and the universe that I had been led to embrace. It was tender, gentle, compassionate writing. Whenever I would write, the heat and energy running through me would be intense, there would be the familiar high-pitched sound in my ears, the fluttering around my face and arms, and a compelling sense that I must write. Throughout, Nicky's own input was enormous, refining, challenging, encouraging.

I began to share what I was writing in the groups to which I belonged, and felt urged to set up a Facebook page, The Therapist in my Pocket, on which to begin to share this writing more widely. The stories and observations clearly reached those who read them in a profound way, and touched hearts and lives. And always there was – and is – the sense of being guided to write the things I write, in the way in which I write them. My room is always filled with orbs of light, joyfully whizzing around in all directions, and it has been wonderful to be able to capture them on video to share with friends all over the globe who understand their meaning and significance.

Eventually, there was so much material that it became clear that this should become a book. That thought was scary, and felt like a huge and daunting task, but Nicky was utterly convinced that this was all meant to be, and gently but very firmly pushed me to contact a publisher.

I believe that this, then, finally, is the book that was meant to be written. It carries the energy of the joy and love that filled that tiny room in the cottage in Derbyshire. It is imbued with the sparkles and shimmers that fill the air still, and the tinkling bells and whispered voices of those who urged, in no uncertain terms, that it should be written. It is carried on the wave of joyous enthusiasm and support of friends all over the world who have enjoyed its contents during the past three months during which I have been writing. And it has the joyous approval of the orbs of light which I know helped to write it.

I invite you to put on this pair of magic spectacles with me, and journey together as we come to explore the wonder, the beauty and the magic of what it means to be 'Dancers Amongst the Stars.'

Love and sparkles!

Tapestry

· ·

We are creating a tapestry,
weaving in and out of
each other's' awareness
with the threads
which are the
patterns of our lives.
And as we tread softly
in and out and
amongst and through,
we gently bow
and touch souls
in recognition
of countless remembered
sacred encounters,
and murmur
'Namaste.'

Molly

· ·

I want to tell you a story. It is a bit of a fairy tale, I suppose.

It is the story of a woman called Molly, but could just as easily be about a woman called Kate, or a man called Sam, or Thomas.

Are you sitting comfortably? Then I will begin…

There was once a little girl called Molly. She was a very lucky little girl. She had a very busy and successful daddy, who worked very hard so that her family could have lots of expensive treats and holidays and presents. She also had a very busy mummy, who was always organizing things, helping other people, here, there and everywhere. Everyone loved her mummy, because she was always so helpful and kind. Molly knew that these were very important things that her mummy and daddy had to do, and so she knew she must not mind. She knew that to mind was being selfish, and made her a bad person. So Molly grew up learning how to be good. Very good.

When Molly was all grown up, she realized that she knew how to be good, but that she did not know how to be happy. She asked her dad, who told her, 'Get yourself a good job, earn lots of money, get yourself a big house and fancy car, and you will be happy.' So Molly tried that. However, although she did everything her dad had suggested, she *still* did not know how to be happy. In fact, she felt a bit empty and a bit lonely. So Molly asked her mum, to see if she could tell her. Her mum said, 'Serve others, always be there whenever anyone needs you. You will be tired, and there will not be time to do things for yourself, but people will love you for it, and so you will be happy.' So Molly tried this. Still she did not feel happy. In fact, truth be told, she felt a bit cross. So Molly went to see her doctor, and told him that she wanted to be happy. Her doctor suggested she take a little white tablet once a day for six months. She did as he suggested, and it made her feel a little calmer, maybe, but once she stopped taking them, she felt just as unhappy as before.

A friend suggested to Molly that she read some self-help books, and so she went out and bought some. The books told her to write loving letters to herself, and to look at herself in the mirror and tell herself that she was beautiful. Molly tried very hard to do this. However, every time she sat down to write herself a loving letter, she could not think what there was to love. And every time she looked into her eyes in the mirror, and tried to say aloud the words the books suggested, the words felt hollow, ridiculous, like they were meant for someone else. Someone more worthy. More loveable.

One day, Molly found herself walking through a forest. It was a path she had never come across before. In fact, she had no idea how she got there. She had just sort of closed her eyes and become very still. She had found herself just listening to herself breathing. And that had brought her here. As she walked along the mossy path through the trees, she noticed a Wise Woman. Just sitting, looking at her. Almost expectantly. She decided there was nothing to lose. And so she went towards the Wise Woman. As she came closer, she could feel a strange energy, tingling through her body. In an inexplicable way, she knew it was an energy that she and the Wise Woman shared. She knew that they were meant to meet here.

The Wise Woman looked at her and waited for her to speak. 'I want to find happiness,' Molly said. 'I don't know what to do to be happy.' The Wise Woman said a strange thing. She said, 'My child, what do you need?' Molly was puzzled, and felt a bit cross. Firstly, the Wise Woman had called her a child. And she was not a child. She was a grown up. Could the Wise Woman not *see* that? Also, the Wise

Woman had asked her what she needed! How useless was that! Did she not realize that she had come here to understand what to *do*, not to be asked what she needed? The Wise Woman saw her reaction, and just smiled. And waited. Molly realized that she was being invited to say something. So she thought hard, and then she said, 'I need to stop *needing* so much!'

The Wise Woman considered, head on one side for several moments. Then she asked, 'what is it that you need, my child, that you feel is too much?' Molly was flabbergasted. She felt like she was being criticized, got at; she felt stupid. Why did the Wise Woman keep asking the same question? She had given her the answer already. Wasn't she listening! Then something clicked. She gasped, as if a shock had gone through her. She looked at the Wise Woman, and looked into kindly, knowing eyes. The Wise Woman smiled and nodded. And waited. Molly looked at her again, then looked away, and then back at her. She saw a depth of knowing in those eyes. Somehow, they gave her courage. She took a deep breath, and began:

'I need to be *loved*.' She said, almost in a whisper. She looked at the Wise Woman for approval, but the Wise Woman just smiled, met her gaze, and waited. 'I need to be *listened* to...and *heard*.'....... Again, the waiting, and the encouraging smile. Suddenly, she knew she could say it all. All of it. All the needing and the wanting, the longings she had kept in for so long: 'I need to say what I'm *feeling*....I need to be allowed to *feel* what I *feel*......I need to not feel guilty......or ashamed......or bad. I need to know I'm *okay*. Just as I *am*. To love *me*!' The words were starting to tumble out now. 'I need to laugh out loud...to be noisy...to enjoy myself...to say yes...to say no...To choose...'

The Wise Woman still met her eyes. Molly stopped and felt the connection. It was so profound that it took her breath away. Then the Wise Woman spoke, very quietly, almost lovingly. The compassion in her voice was so soothing, such a relief, like balm on a sore wound. 'My child, you have *always* needed to do those things. They were *always* yours.

To experience them was the reason you came. But you had forgotten, and now you have remembered. When we fall into a place of forgetting, we forget our joy, our power, our magnificence, our freedom. And in its place, we learn shame. You have learned to feel ashamed for being you, my child. You must forgive yourself.'

Again, the surprise at what the Wise Woman had said. Molly thought and thought, but could not understand. 'I don't understand,' she said. The Wise Woman nodded. It was clear that she did not need any further explanation. That she knew what Molly meant.

'When we forget who we are, and why we came here, we start to believe we have got things badly wrong, have done things that make us bad. We feel terrible shame. We stop being able to be ourselves, still less to love ourselves. Instead, there is only shame.'

'You have to forgive yourself for forgetting, my child. For allowing shame to take over. For hating and despising yourself.'

Molly thought about the Wise Woman's words. At first, they sounded extreme but, the more she pondered, she noticed a growing feeling inside her that said the words were true. 'What must I do?' she asked. 'What would you *like* to do?' the Wise Woman asked her. Softly. Like she, too, was holding her breath. Slowly, meaningfully, Molly stood up. 'I would like to laugh...and shout...and dance...and run...and splash in puddles! I want to say it like it is, no more pretending, I want to choose, to change, to be free, to be me!'.....' *Me!* 'She was shouting now. And grinning. And laughing. Arms wide, head thrown back.

Suddenly, she became aware that the Wise Woman was no longer there. She felt bereft, as if a part of her was missing. 'Where are you?' she cried out. 'Don't leave me now. Not now. I've only just begun to know you.' Somewhere, she could not tell whether it came from inside her or outside of her, she *felt* a voice. As it spoke, it seemed to vibrate all through her. The air around her sparkled and shimmered. 'You haven't lost me, my child. You can never lose me, nor I you. We are forever one, always were, always will be. You need only listen, and you will remember.'

Then she heard a peel of laughter, bright, sparkly, effervescent, full and joyous. It was like a thousand bells tinkling. The air was full. What of, Molly could not tell, but somehow she again felt a remembering stir in her. 'But for now, beloved child of mine, you need to go and jump in some puddles!'

So she did!

The gift

· ·

When you can hold up
for another soul
the mirror of your
own tenderness
till they can see
their own beauty
reflected there,
you have bestowed
on that soul
a gift
of unimaginable love
and your souls
will never forget

Toddler in the courtyard

· ·

The other day, I was sitting in a courtyard outside a tea shop, enjoying the sunshine and the general comings and goings of what is a beautiful place, when my attention was caught by a small family group sitting just back from me and to my left. It was a man and woman, a young child and a toddler, maybe twenty months old or so. The family were having some cake and drinks, and a collie dog approached and was clearly curious, sniffing the toddler as he sat in his buggy and wagging his tail.

The toddler was transfixed, then excited, and clearly wanted to say hello.

He reached out and patted the dog, a bit clumsily, as toddlers do, and the dog responded. He moved closer and gave the toddler's hand a lick. The toddler wriggled in delight, and his dad noticed, and encouraged him, saying what a lovely dog it was, and how nice it was to make friends and say hello. The toddler visibly expanded, reveling in this new friendship. Grinning from ear to ear, he patted and stroked the collie, talking to him animatedly in his way, and receiving happy licks and tail wags back, as these two formed a quite beautiful bond. The world was a friendly, fun place where you reach out to other souls and they reach right back.

Then, this little person suddenly had a new idea. You could see it register. The deliciousness of it. He would share some of his food with his new friend! He broke off a piece of his cake, and held it out to the dog, smiling. With infinite tenderness, the dog very gently came forward to a position where he could take the offered food with his tongue so as not to risk catching the infant's fingers with his teeth. The moment was magical. The infant was giving something of his own, that he was able to give, and his friend was accepting it.

And then, the infant's dad noticed. In the same moment, the infant realized that his dad had seen, and grinned expectantly at him, expecting him to share the wonder of what was happening. Just like he had before when the dog had first come over.

However, his dad said, in a voice full of urgency and anxiety, 'Don't do that! He might bite you!'

The toddler's face startled, then crumpled, and then his whole body collapsed, and he let out the biggest howl of a painful sob you have ever heard. And when he had his breath back from that first sob, he just sobbed and sobbed again. He was inconsolable. The dog slunk away, confused. The little boy cried and cried, and did not know how to stop. His parents tried to distract him, showed him toys, tried to get him to laugh, offered him more of the cake, but all he could do was sob.

In the end, his mother picked him up out of the buggy he was sitting in, cuddled him to her, and walked away from the table and out of the courtyard. You could still hear him crying for a good ten to fifteen minutes.

Years ago, when I was a psychotherapist in training, one of the most emotionally challenging aspects of that training was a two-year child observation. We observed a child, and that child's interactions with the world, every week for two years. We were trained to look and really see. To see the meaning, to notice what was going on in that child's internal and external world, and watch how that child's developing self was affected by those experiences. To respond emotionally to the *detail*. For those of us who were parents, it was such a revelation, a privilege like no other opportunity ever, before or since, a chance to really *see*. And what had just happened reminded me of so many instances observed during that child observation where we, as grownups, well intentioned as we most certainly usually are, ride rough shod over a child's emerging world so thoroughly that we spoil something that cannot easily be retrieved.

Now, some onlookers, watching that scene, would have felt that the father was absolutely right to say what he said. He had not wanted his son to be bitten by the dog. But of-course, the father was not really looking. The dog's body language was in no way aggressive, and both child and dog were being careful of each other. Other onlookers might have decided that the little boy was having a tantrum. That he was objecting to not being allowed to do what he wanted. They would possibly even say that he wanted his own way and was spoiled, needed to be shown he could not have everything he wanted. Others looking on might decide that the mother was making way too much of it all, taking him away and cuddling him for all that time. That it would teach him to do the same another time, showing him how to get his own way.

All these things you would find people thinking. We are brought up and conditioned to believe that children know no better, that they have no inner wisdom of their own, that the 'grown up' view of the world and how it operates is self-evidently the correct one. However, when we do that, we miss the point. Just as that father missed the point. We miss the glorious truth that our children come into the world to teach *us*, and not the other way round.

However, if you listened, really listened, with empathy, care, and openness, to the quality of the sobs coming from that little body, you would have known that it was not about any of those things that people not really listening might have decided it was. Because the thing you would have heard, right there in the midst of those heart-rending sobs, would have been *grief*. And once you had heard the grief, you might find your own feelings stirred. You might find yourself experiencing flickers of long lost memory, of when you too were newly here, of when you still knew you were a spark of Source energy coming on an adventure, of when you still remembered the place where we all shared the same heart and were One, of when you still knew that we were all Love. A time before the adults around you introduced you to fear.

That is what was in the sobs. That was the overwhelming grief. That was the loss.

We do that to each other all the time, do we not? The word of caution, the hesitation in our voice, the warning, the frown, the look of disapproval or anxiety or dismay. We perpetuate the myth that fear is the correct way, the sensible way, the self-protective way, the way the world is. But just supposing we gave it a try, this other way. The way that this little boy sitting in his buggy offering some of his food to that dog came to remind us of, to show us all over again. Just supposing we did that.
Wow, what a world this could be!

If not you

· ·

Gently, with
infinite tenderness
and compassion
raw and from
the heart,
hold the child
that was you
in the palm
of your hand,
and send them
all the love
they need
to feel
in order
to feel safe
and understood
and worthy
and loved
and to be free
to move on.
Then wrap them up
tight
deep within your heart
and bring
them home.
If not you,
then who?

Oneness

· ·

I was walking through a shopping center the other day when I became aware, afresh and startlingly, of just how much eye contact was going on between people who were apparently total strangers. I am not meaning brief glances, or furtive looks. I mean full-blown eye-to-eye exchanges that held warmth and familiarity and a knowingness. People shared so much in those wordless communications, far more than they might have been immediately conscious of. They passed each other by having shared how their day was going, how they were feeling, what was on their mind. Mostly, they probably would not have given the exchange any further thought. Nevertheless, that exchange would always have happened and, even if they never thought of it again, they would have touched each other's lives.

But it was something more than this that I was noticing. Something even more profound. It was the *recognition* in the eyes. You will, I am sure, have experienced it yourself. A total stranger looks you straight in the eyes and beams at you as if they know you. Not in any intrusive or inappropriate way; just a direct gaze or a beaming smile that leaves you wondering how you know each other, where or when you have met before. A wonderful moment of soul-to-soul recognition.

In addition, that noticing led me to think just how stunning, how breathe taking, how full of aliveness, the eyes are. How much we see and receive through them. The depth of what is held there. How much is so powerfully and yet so subtly communicated through our eyes. And how, so very often, we will see reflected back to us in the eyes of a complete stranger, as we pass each other by in what is sometimes the smallest, briefest of encounters, something of our own soul, our own being.

A long time ago, I worked for a number of years teaching therapists in training, and one exercise that we would do with everyone very early on never ceased to amaze us. The students - maybe fifty or more - would be asked to walk in and out of each other, moving around freely, making eye contact with anyone with whom they felt drawn to do so. Then, after about five minutes or so, they were asked to approach someone, just one person, with whom they had experienced a special pull, a sense of a bond, and to then spend a little time together sharing some information about their past and current lives. Without exception, always the similarities were striking, to the point of seeming uncanny. Students would always find themselves shaken by how much of ourselves we can see in another, simply through the eyes, without a word being spoken.

Many years later, with fresh insights and new awareness, I realize that this exercise was, of-course, confirming just how true it is that we are all mirrors of each other. *For* each other. Back then, I would have understood this recognition as a form of identification: what we see in another is always a part of ourselves. That part is often a disavowed aspect of us, one that we only see through it being made manifest in another. But however that may be, what it confirms every single time is our common humanity. That we are *the same.*

Now, I use a different language. I may no longer call this phenomenon 'identification.' However, the fundamental truth remains: The Divine, Source, All That Is, or whatever you wish to call the creative force from which everything flows, receives the world and gives to the world very powerfully through the *eyes.* This energy, this *Beingness*, holds everything in its tender embrace, sees and feels all, shares and experiences all, *is* all.

You immediately recognize those who are in touch with this energy, because their eyes are radiant with love and peace and joy. They are the eyes you do not want to look away from kind of eyes. They hold you in a very particular spell and bathe you in what feels like an eternal and loving embrace. Something stirs deep inside you, a kind of remembering. You may not be able to formulate it, but you have seen it, and you have felt it viscerally. You know you have been touched by the Divine. And that what you have just encountered is the Divine present in a fellow soul.

When you look into the eyes of those who are in touch with who they really are, who are simply in the flow of that beautiful energy, you find yourself suddenly dissolving into your own divine essence too. You suddenly find yourself transported somewhere else, to a dimension where the things which have come to seem so important, the stuff of life as you have been living it, dissolves for a moment. You find yourself, however briefly, seeing past all the illusion, all the self-importance and paranoia of the ego. Instead, you recognize your own spark of divinity, and you find yourself experiencing the same love, peace, joy, contentment that you have just seen reflected back to you. It is one of those wonderful moments that reminds you that there is something else, something more. That *you* are something else, something more. You have a sense that you have grown taller, bigger, more powerful, and your heart swells.

Once you have become attuned to the way this can happen, you become increasingly tuned in also to the way in which the Divine reveals itself by appearing in the eyes of others. And the more you see it, the more you find yourself recognizing those who have already grasped the most beautiful secret: that we are all One. It is Oneness that you have seen when you have been caught in one of those profound moments of recognition. You can barely grasp it, because it is so fleeting. You have seen who you really are, and you have seen yourself in the eyes of another who, maybe for the briefest of seconds, saw reflected back at them through your eyes who they really are.

We are all part of this same energy, there is no difference between us; we are different versions of each other, but the same energy. When those magical moments happen, we realize, with the most wonderful shock of recognition, that there is always only ever one Being present, taking an infinite variety of forms. And that this Being is *who we are*. We all notice this, every one of us, all the time. We may not be able to put these words to it, or formulate it in this way. Nevertheless, we feel a knowing, a recognition, or a remembering without being able to work out quite what it was. Try looking out for it, intentionally; it happens everywhere, all the time, far more than you might think. Total strangers look into each other's eyes, as they pass by in the street, or in a shopping queue, or in a café, or a doctor's waiting room. We recognize both our shared humanity and our shared divinity; we see our Oneness.

The delicious truth is that, if you let them, eyes can actually bring you *home* to the essence which is you.

We come home in the eyes of another, and also in our own eyes in a mirror. If we look deeply enough and for long enough we see Source gazing back at us. We have to see past all the self-judgment and self-hatred, the sense of ugliness and unworthiness. We have to look long enough. But eventually, if we keep gazing into our own eyes, we will see beyond, and the eyes that we realize are looking back into ours will have changed. The eyes we now see are always steady, loving, without judgment, fully accepting, of all we are. Look long enough, deeply enough, and you will see the mask of the ego dissolve and melt away. All you will see in its place is the glorious alive awareness that we all truly are. And love. Always the most incredible love.

Oneness shines in the eyes of everyone. Look for it and you will see it. Know it, and you will allow others to see it too, in you. And once we have seen it, we can never see anything else!

Let Go

Let go
of your thoughts....
of your opinions....
even of your name
and who you think you are...
Give up trying to be separate,
to compete, to succeed, to win.
Instead, embrace not knowing.
Be willing to be disturbed,
to discover that you were wrong.
To be taken apart
and put back together again.
Look and see.
And see more.

Letter from an Animal Guide

. . . .

"Dear human

Sometimes we in the animal realms look on and shake our heads at the stark staring obviousness of what you so easily miss. Sometimes we even cover our eyes so we don't have to watch. But I've been elected - and I tell you, it was a long and heated discussion, because none of us wanted the job - to try to set you straight on a few things. So I'm going to give it my best shot. I'm hoping you'll get what I'm saying, but from your track record so far, I'm not holding my breath. So anyway, here goes:

This law of attraction stuff some of you keep harping on about, it's so simple we don't get why you find it so hard to grasp. We animals do it all the time. And we don't 't even *think* about it.

Okay, okay, see this is what I *thought* would happen. I told them. I said you'd start shouting me down. I told them. I said, you know how it'll go, they'll start quoting at me. They'll start listening in order to reply rather than *really* listening. And they said, but we have to try, don't we? They said, we know their ego is going to get in the way, and they're going to be convinced they know better. They said, we know their ego is going to make them want to tell you it's more complicated than that, and we agree that their ego thing is what stresses us animal guides out more than anything else about our humans, but hey, give it a go. Just give it a go. They said.

So can you just at least *try* to listen? Just for five minutes. It won't take long, I promise, and then you can go back to your intellectual stuff - which, has to be said, seems to us such a total waste of time, but I'm not supposed to say that because they said it would get your backs up, so I won't - and then when I've said it I can get back to my job of trying to keep you humans from messing up. Okay? Deal?

So here goes. We animals live in what we call 'The Flow.' We *live in* it. It's not something outside of us, we don't *make* it happen. The Flow simply *is*. The Flow meets our every need, and we don't spend any time worrying about tomorrow or beating ourselves up about, or crying over, yesterday. That truth takes away all stress, all angst, for us. We know The Flow is. We know The Flow is abundant. We know the Flow always takes care. We take what we need and are never greedy for more. We watch the world going by, but always know we are in The Flow and not of this world we observe......oh, surprised you, that bit, didn't it? You thought we weren't that clever, huh? Well, duh.

You humans *also* live in The Flow. It's not outside of you. It simply *is*. But because of this crazy ego thing you have - oh, oops, sorry, I'm not supposed to use judgmental words - you seem to think that you're outside of it. And because you think you're outside of it, you don't get that it just *is*, you develop this striving thing that we animals just can't understand. See, you don't *need* to strive. You don't need to *try*. You don't need to compete, or be the best, or try to show how special you are, or try to prove you can control the universe by thinking certain things. Stuff like this Law of Attraction thing you have going.

I want to tell you a secret: we animals have a different word for it. We don't get all technical. We have a saying. Whenever any of us meet each other, we simply murmur, 'We are in The Flow.' Now that's pretty sacred to us, that saying. It is how we greet each other, and how we take leave of each other. Before we take life, we say to the one who gives their life to us, 'We are in The Flow.' We say it with appreciation, with gratitude. And we don't take that life until the one who is giving their life has replied back, 'We are in The Flow.' We know we come from The Flow, that we go back to The Flow. That The Flow is in us and around us and in all things. That we *are* The Flow, as are all things. And before we choose to incarnate - just as you do - we visualize how our brief time here on this earth plane is going to go. We do it briefly, and quickly, because we know by now how pretty insignificant that all is in the overall scheme of things, in the life of The Flow. We know that we will live out what we agreed, and that it will always be going the way it needs to be going. And we know we are always being taken care of by The Flow. That everything is always working out.

See, if only you humans could get that. Really get that. But you cut yourselves off from The Flow by choosing to do the thinking thing. If you would only use your senses, as we animals do, it could all be so simple. Because I tell you, when you allow yourself to be in The Flow, life is joyous and peaceful and worry free. You don't *make* law of attraction work, you *allow* law of attraction to work. Life is *always* working out for you because, just as we animals do, you *planned* how it would go before you came. So you don't have to *make* it happen, because it's already *going* to happen. You simply have to *allow* it and enjoy the ride, this time around. When you simply allow, you will always find happiness. Always. There. So that's it. You just have to let go, allow, appreciate, be joyous and curious, and go with The Flow, in The Flow. When you do that, everything you spend so much time reading and talking about will *happen* for you. Because you'll be *in the flow*.

Okay, so, thanks for listening. I'm going to find me a shady tree now and lay under it for a while. After that, I'll see what takes my fancy. Just going with The Flow.

See you around x"

Love's Tears

Love said to me, 'Look up.'
But I shook my head.
Love asked me
why I would not meet her eyes.
I said I was unworthy.
Love asked me what made me so.

And I told Love
all that I had done
and had failed to do.
All I had got wrong,
all I had failed to understand.
How I hated, and resented,
how hard it was for me
to get past my hurts and let go.
I whispered my shame.
And as I did so, my cheeks burned.

And Love lifted my chin
and kissed my cheek,
oh so infinitely tenderly.
But still I did not dare look up.
So Love kissed my head,
just there, as I was.
And still I would not look up.
Love stroked my hair
and told me that nothing

in all the universe
was more loveable than I was.
Or more worthy and deserving.

The shock of her words
made me lift my head.
To see.
And yet, looking, I saw nothing.
But I felt my cheek wet,
and knew that these were Love's own tears.

At first I did not understand.
Shame still burned, but
something else burned also.
A different fire, cleansing,
hotter than the shame,
and much deeper, right in the core of me.
And suddenly I perceived,
beyond my shame, a fresher reality.
I no longer was my shame;
rather, I saw my shame.
I was the one watching, experiencing,
knowing, learning, expanding.

And suddenly, where there had been only
me, alone and separate and judging,
there was now a new me,
embracing all in compassion and wisdom.
Including all the doing and the failing,
and the shame.

And I remembered Love,
I could see her face again,
smiling through tears at my remembering.
And I wondered

how I had ever thought
I could not look up.
Or that I was not worthy.
Or undeserving of love.
And I realized that the tears
on my cheeks were not mine only,
but were the tears of thousands,
just as, also, was the shame
and the failure, the pain and the hurt.
I remembered. Oh, I remembered!

And I stood up, in my full power,
human and divine.

And, laughing out loud at it all,
I finally looked up.

Trust

· ·

If you were asked if you trust life, I wonder what your answer would be. The answer might be immediately obvious to you, because the feeling that rises in you in response to that question is very clear. Alternatively, it might take you a while to ponder and consider. It might be a new thought, something you have not ever really considered before. Take your time, and think about it.

Do you say yes, because you trust that life is always bringing you exactly what experience you need in any given moment? That you know all is well no matter what is happening right now, or no matter how it might appear? Or do you say no, and that you feel that everything is completely unknown and unpredictable, and you do not like the feeling of being out of control? Maybe you talk about Fate. You might say that Fate seems to deal some people a good hand and others a not so good one. That it is the luck of the draw? Do you perhaps say that most of the time you do trust life, but you do find it comforting to seek out psychic readings and other methods of seeing into the future because it's nice to know what the future holds? Just to be sure? Or maybe something different entirely?

It is an important question, because the way we view life determines how we engage with our life, and the way we choose to live it. It leads us, for instance, to either feel that we can jump in wholeheartedly to the opportunities life presents us with, because everything will be okay. Or it leads us to feel we want to hold back and to see guarantees before we make a move. Or it leads us to live in 'if only', and look on through the window at life going on for others, wishing we could go inside and join them but never quite finding the courage to do that. Our response to that question also determines how we deal with troubles or apparent setbacks. I suspect many of us live our lives in more fear than we would maybe easily acknowledge to ourselves. Even those of us who would say that we were on a spiritual journey of self-discovery, and who were coming to realize just how much we influence the particular reality in which we exist, have a wobble now and then.

We like the words, 'things are always working out for me' and 'you are always exactly where you need to be,' that we hear so often amongst 'enlightened' friends and spiritual writers and teachers. We like the words a lot, and we would *love* to believe that they are true wholeheartedly. Really, we would. And we say them religiously day after day, several times a day, as affirmations or mantras. We try incredibly hard! But our history and experience of life to date seems to so easily contradict that. And so, perfectly understandably, we get scared. I want to say 'perfectly understandably' because this is not about getting you to beat yourself up for your fears. Rather, it is about suggesting that, even in that place of fearfulness, you are doing what you came here to do. You are completely on track. This is not the way it seems. How about we go and visit the big picture for a few moments, and remind ourselves why we are here. Why we came.

We came here, as sparks of Source energy, to experience life in a human, physical form. We came for expansion. Source is always expanding. Forget anything you have heard about 'it should be easy.' That is just going to make you beat yourself up and believe you are getting it wrong when you hit those times when it is not feeling particularly easy. And sometimes it just *is* that way. So what is this thing we refer to as expansion? How does Source expand? Why does Source need to expand at all?

Source expands because that is the nature of love. And Source is Love. Source expands through the love and compassion which experiencing the whole range and extent of human joy and pain, fear and excitement, tension and release brings. It can be no other way. And *you* are Source energy, and so *you* came to do that.

Knowing that changes things a lot, if we allow it to! When we get fearful while looking through the eyes of our ego - the bit of us that holds us together while we're getting used to how this ride goes - we can start to believe that life is dangerous and unpredictable, and we retreat from the greater truths we could get in touch with if we kept our hearts open, instead of shutting them down. Those greater truths include the fact that we all chose the key elements of what experiences we would welcome in this lifetime, as Source energy, in the service both of our own expansion and the expansion of All That Is.

We did not choose how we would react or respond - that is the bit that is about expansion. That is the journey and the challenge and the adventure of this lifetime. And it is easier once we embrace it rather than fighting it. Because then we can say, and understand the enormity of it, 'everything is always working out for me' or 'I am exactly where I need to be.' We can say that because we have grasped firmly that we are an integral and essential part of everything else, that we are not doing this separately or on our own, but as part of a web of energy and expanding love that never ceases to become more. We can then take fully on board that, as Source energy, we are on a mission.

We are on the leading edge. And our journey, and what we choose to do with it, is being shared by more loving light energy and supportive presence than we can ever imagine, and that there is more profound wisdom and extraordinary power available to us in any given moment than we can begin to comprehend from this earthly perspective.

We can then begin to understand that those statements we say so readily are actually the statements of a powerful creator who has chosen to have a complex and expansive and fully human experience. A real experience, a full experience, an unconditional one. In Love and with compassion and loads and loads of help and support. And once we get that, everything changes. We have moved from powerless unwilling victim to powerful and willing creator. And our relationship with Source shifts perspective too. We no longer expend endless effort trying to work out what prayers or rituals or affirmations we can use to persuade Source to make it different. We stand tall and know that we are a trailblazer, that we came because we were strong enough to play this role, see this out, make good sense of it and use it, grow in understanding and compassion, and joy and love through it, and mindfully, as co-creators, give that back to Source as glorious expansion. Because we *are* Source and the expansion is who we are becoming.

Do you see how different that is? Do you feel the excitement of the enormity of it! Can you feel the expansion of it already? So how about we go forward knowing that this is who we are, why we are, all we are? How about we remember where we came from and where we go back to, and who we remain all the time in between? How about we go forward in our full power, knowing all we have, all that surrounds us, all that is loving us and supporting us, sharing the wisdom and strength of all that is breathing every breath with us and looking through our eyes with us every single step we take, and expanding with every emotion we feel and every thought and perception we have?

How about we just do that!

Remember

. . . .

When we look
into the eyes
of another
we see ourselves
reflected there,
and we realize
with the shock
and pang
and compassion
born of remembering,
that there
is only one
Being here

Helen

· ·

I heard a comment the other day. It is one I have heard a lot through my life, and one I have used myself in the past on several occasions too. It is one of the most damning things one human being can say about another. It is a write-off comment. A throw your hands up in the air and shake your head kind of comment. It is an 'I wash my hands of you' comment. A 'there is no hope for you' comment. An 'I can't do this anymore' kind of comment.

Know what that is? It is this: 'They're a bottomless pit.'

We all know what that means, don't we? And the kind of person it describes. The 'bottomless pit' person. It is the 'nothing is ever enough' kind of person. The 'I always need more' kind of person. The person who seems to be unable to hold onto anything you have offered. Who begs you to say something helpful or comforting one day, but then needs you to say it all over again the following day, and the next. And the next. The person who cannot seem to find a way to use anything you say to them, anything you give them. To *hold* anything.

That is what we mean, is it not, when we call them a 'bottomless pit'? We say things like 'They just take, take, take.' Or, 'There's no point in trying to help because it won't make a blind bit of difference!' And we shake our head and walk away feeling pretty self-satisfied and self-righteous. We have done the best we can, we have given and given, and this person is just ungrateful, no longer deserving. In fact, a dead loss.

That *is* what we mean, isn't it, by 'A bottomless pit.' Damning indeed.

So how about, just for a moment, we walk in the shoes of a 'bottomless pit'? How about we just peek at what that is like? We won't stay there too long, because we will want to shake those shoes off pretty quickly, and to breathe a sigh of relief that we do not have to wear them all the time. However, let's just give it a go? Just to make it a little easier, I am going to give this 'bottomless pit' a name. How about we call her 'Helen'? It just makes it simpler to give her a human face for a while.

So, let's put on Helen's shoes.

The world, for Helen, is a really frightening place. It started out that way. Helen's mum was not really cut out for mothering. She did not have very much of anything to give to a baby apart from practical care - given in a no-nonsense kind of way - because she had not had it herself. So, inside, Helen's mum was a bottomless pit too, hungry for what she had not had, resentful of being required to give what she had not had to someone else. In fact, if the truth were told, Helen's mum was even a bit envious of her little girl. Why should Helen be the centre of the universe when she, the mother, had never been given that?

Helen's mum lived life as if it owed her. She believed that Helen owed her, too. Helen was her second chance. Helen should give her everything that her own mother had been unable to give her. Note: unable. We are not blaming anyone here. It was as it was. It is as it is. We are just putting on another pair of shoes, remember.

Fairly early on in Helen's life, therefore, Helen learned that she came second. She learned that she did not deserve. She learned that good things were not for her. She learned that life was not kind, or comforting, or soothing, or giving. Rather, life was punishing, taking, and begrudging. Moreover, life expected that she should not mind. But something even harder came with that. Helen grew up unable to *hold* anything. In therapy speak, to contain anything. It is complicated. One of the greatest of human pains there is. She grew up *empty*.

Let's imagine that for a moment. Some of us will already know what this means, because we already know what that is like. It feels frightening. Joyless. It means to be untouched by anything good, to be unable to remember it, or conjure up the feeling of it. Everything is fleeting and temporary. It goes in but it just falls right out again. People who know it often refer to it as 'the void.'

See, we can only hold onto things if *we* have been held. If our being mothered has included our being physically, emotionally, psychologically held. If we have felt and known that we were existing in another's heart and mind. We only know *we* exist because we first discovered that we existed in the heart and mind of *another*. So moments vanish. Others' words vanish. At least, 'good' moments do. And 'good' words do. 'Bad' moments stay because there is no way to soothe them. And 'bad' words stay because they are all we have known, so they are familiar and trusted.

Do you begin to see the pain of the 'bottomless pit' yet?

Oh, it does not end there. It gets worse. As an adult, Helen continues to feel like a hungry, needy child. Just like her mother was. She feels so bad about that, so ashamed, so inadequate. She hates and despises herself. She is a horrible person for being so full of hurt and anger and resentment. And the worse she feels about herself, the more she tries to compensate by being 'good.'

Helen usually cares for her mother, often lives with her longer than many daughters live with their mothers, or continues to live close by. She tries hard to meet her every need, and resents all she has to do for her, while believing that she is bad for resenting it. Neither mother nor daughter are happy in this arrangement, there is duty here, not love. Although both would insist on *calling* it love. Both believe it is love. Neither really know what this thing called love actually is. Now and then, Helen goes through periods of the darkest, most desolate, depression. She will catapult between anger and grief. She will cry for days. She will walk out. She will shout 'cruel' things. Then she will be overcome by guilt and remorse. And shame. Oh, always the shame.

When it gets really bad, she will ask for help. She is clearly in so much distress that others are eager to try to help her. People give her hugs, words of encouragement, practical offers of help. And Helen expresses her gratitude and appears to absorb it all and feel better. People feel gratified and content that their help has made a difference. However, in Helen's world, all it has actually been is a sticking plaster. It has helped temporarily. But the void - the bottomless pit - remains. Everything is just as hollow, empty, frightening, and meaningless as before. She is still a 'bad' person and she still hates herself. She genuinely tries to do the things she has been advised to do. She reads the books. The writes love letters to herself. She says affirmations as if they are sacred, magic rituals that will bring about lasting healing, even though she knows she doesn't deserve it. She tries to love herself like everyone tells her to do. But always, there is the void, always the bottomless pit. Always the inability to *hold* it. And so it gets even worse. People start to get angry with her. They tell her she is not trying. They bombard her with wise words which others have spoken or written. They tell her to snap out of it. Or to look to her vibration. To change her energy. They tell her she is attracting this.

Do you get yet what it is like to be Helen? Yet?

And do you know the only way it gets fixed? The *only* way? The way that someone who doesn't know how to love themselves gets to be able to love themselves? It is by being given, over and over again, the unconditional love they did not have. That does not mean depleting yourself. It does not mean giving in a way that leaves you empty. However, it does mean not telling her to do what she simply cannot do - no matter how loudly and clearly and impatiently you tell her to do it.

And now do you see the challenge? Both for Helen, and also for you? Do you see why Helen chose - because, of-course, she *did* choose - to bring this opportunity into this time/space reality for us all? Do you see what a strong soul Helen actually is? Do you see what she offers *you*? It is the challenge of finding a way to love unconditionally. To give unconditionally. To find in yourself all the blocks to unconditional love which the difficult personality that Helen is forcing you to discover.

This never *was* about Helen. This never *was* about the frustration of the bottomless pit. This was never about you learning wonderful techniques that you could offer to Helen in order to help her to be like you. It was *always* about *you*. And for that, you owe Helen enormous appreciation. Helen has already got this. She knew what she was doing. She has this. Her higher self is looking on, smiling, and nodding at the absolutely brilliant job she is doing of playing out her role. Her bottomless pit role. Don't you just love that! And do you get it now? Even a little? The enormity of this gift?

The challenge is unconditional love. The opportunity is unconditional love. The journey is unconditional love. Do you catch the energy of that, the excitement of it, the power of it? Don't you just love the way this all works?

Oh, and if you happen to be Helen, thank you! There is much love and appreciation for you here! We stand in awe!

Whispers on the Wind

· ·

I am listening
to the whispers on the Wind.
Maybe you can hear them too?
Quietly, softly, the tenderest breath.
The whispers down the years,
echoing and sighing,
laughing and joyous,
weeping and grieving,
pondering and wondering,
asking and offering,
meeting and taking leave.
And, as I listen,
I hear words.
They are speaking,
I realize,
to me.
It is in the smallest of whispers,
but I can make out voices,
now, and there, and again, now.
"It was all to bring you
to this place, Beloved.
Every birth, every death,
every encounter, every loss,
every struggle, every triumph.
All for you.
We are the dancers
and the keepers,

who see and know all.
I tried to understand,
and asked, almost not daring
to hope,
"Do you know *me*, then?"
Do you see *me*!"
In answer,
the most joyous
and the most intimate
hug of remembering
greeted me.
In it, more love,
more compassion,
more understanding and knowing
than I could have imagined.
It held me, surrounded me,
but also filled and warmed me.
It became my whole Being,
until that was all there was.
And I *knew*. Oh, I *knew*.
I knew that we were one
and the same.
Many experiences, many lives
and lifetimes.
But one Being. Only. And always.
That they were where I had been,
and was now.
And that I had been where they were,
and would be again.
That time and place had no meaning
for us,
that this is the reality,
this hug,
this holding, this knowing,
this one and the same and this all.

And I walk now
in that knowing,
in their company and with their companionship,
through days that have no end,
just as they had no beginning.
And I know, with all my knowing,
in this beautiful remembering,
that I AM.

Love is energy

. . . .

A song, 'The Water is wide' goes: 'Love is gentle and love is kind.' I used to sing it often to the guitar some years ago, but it is only recently that the truth of those words really made an impact on me. It struck me that, usually, when we talk about love, we tend to think of it as being a feeling, an emotion. I always used to think of it that way too.

However, I realize now that Love is so much more than that. It is so much more that a feeling. It is active, dynamic, something that we experience and live with our whole being. We both love and *are* love. Love is a being and a doing. It is a welling up of the deepest parts of us, and an outpouring of all that is contained there, a giving and a receiving. Love reaches out and touches, it offers itself and responds, it is gentle and it is kind. That is its nature. And it is gentleness and kindness. That is its manifestation. That is how we recognize it. Love cares and shows concern; it gives because it can, without needing something back. It simply loves because, quite simply, that is its nature. Love listens, caresses, nourishes, nurtures, empowers.

Over the years, I have realized how different real love is to the other phenomenon that we call love, which is not love at all, but need. We use the words love and need interchangeably so readily, especially where romantic love is concerned. But need is so different to true love. Need is based in the illusion that another human being can be our salvation, can somehow complete us, make up for everything we feel is lacking, give us the things we never had, or don't have, make us feel less alone because we do not feel whole in our own company. Need of this kind is a self-centered hunger for something unattainable. That is not a judgmental statement;

it is simply a compassionate observation of a search which many of us can unwittingly get caught up in when we feel alone and incomplete. Far from being kind and gentle and giving, need is more often jealous, controlling, punishing, tortured, possessive, judgmental, consumed. And consuming. It is a state in which true love cannot thrive, can hardly even exist. Need seeks to possess and to control, to limit and to use. It is based on appearances, demands, expectations. It feels entitled in a way that denies the entitlement of the other. It destroys what it hoped to build.

The only way we can freely love is to love simply because we love. To love for love's own sake. To give our love because we choose to give it, and because that is enough. To accept another as being worthy and deserving of love just as they are. And ourselves just as we are. To see Love as who we are, independently of anything it might bring. To love without calculation. To love without keeping score. This is love without condition. Nothing is needed in return, or asked for in return. It is love free of fear. Loving for the joy of loving, just because love is our nature.

That is the kind of love that is transformative. It touches and changes lives, in a look, a touch, a word. It transforms us because it leads us into a deep remembering of who we really are. It is the kind of love that is the most fulfilling experience in the whole world. It also transforms others because, when we are living this kind of love, it radiates out of us, it cannot fail to be seen and felt. It is the greatest gift, even if they do not know why, that we can bestow on another, and it costs us nothing. Rather, it enriches us, and causes us to walk around with a smile on our face and a swelling heart. And everyone who comes into the energy of that ends up walking around with a smile on his or her face and a swelling heart too. It is what we are here to remember, and when we do, we see beauty everywhere. In everyone and everything. We are unstoppable, uplifting, and inspiring, and the energy we radiate ripples out to the furthest corners of the universe.

When we love like that, we change hearts and lives and worlds. We have become once again the creators we always were but had just forgotten briefly. We find we are drawn to others who have also remembered how to love, and in finding them, we meet our destiny and recognize our true refuge. All else dissolves, because it becomes unimportant.

And all that is left is the Love that we are.

Finding Myself

Love said
I am here
But I would not look
Love said
Dare
But I would not reach
Love said
You are beautiful
But I would not hear it
Love said
You are precious
But I would not believe it
Love said
You are afraid
And I nodded
Love said
Close your eyes
Go within
And I closed my eyes
Love said
Remember
And I wept
for joy
at finding
Myself

The Caretakers

. . . .

I am going to share some thoughts with you about what I call, with enormous compassion and love, the Caretaker Personality. I think very many of us will recognize ourselves here, and I hope that recognition will help us to be free. So let me first describe the Caretaker Personality. I am going to refer to her as a she, but she could just as easily be a he. I will call her Ellie.

The caretaker personality does exactly what the name suggests. She takes care of everyone. She gives and gives endlessly, tirelessly. If anyone needs anything, she is right there. If there is a cause to be championed, she will be on the steering committee, if money needs raising, she will put herself through hell to raise the most. She will never say no to you. She will never put herself first. She will neglect herself and her family and immediate loved ones in order to be there for a complete stranger. If she could, she would save the whole world. But you know what? Deep down, it does not do it for her. She is one of the most deeply unhappy and angry women alive. You would never know it, because she would die of shame and be wracked with guilt if you ever suggested it. But this woman, who gives what feels like love to hundreds, struggles to feel loved herself.

Let me tell you a little about the way the woman we are going to call Ellie grew up and what she learned. About people, about life, about herself. It is one of a number of possible scenarios, but is pretty accurate overall. Ellie's Mum was a 'very wonderful woman', who would always do anything for anyone. She was always helping a neighbor out, nursing a sick relative, doing good deeds. It meant there was not always time enough to talk through the little everyday things her kids needed to tell her, or for lots of hugs and stories, but her kids knew that it would be greedy and ungrateful to mind because their mum was a saint. The other important thing to say about Ellie's mum is that she was quite an anxious person. She worried a lot. Ellie learned this from being very young, and knew that if she troubled her mum with any of her problems, her mum would not sleep that night. And Ellie also knew that, if she ever did anything naughty or disappointing, then her mum would be very upset, and the change she saw in her would make her feel like she didn't love her any more.

Ellie's dad was quite emotionally cold, rather shut down, and would become impatient when Ellie's mum would worry endlessly about things, and so Ellie knew not to trouble him, either. And he also had a deep mistrust of the world and other people, and a very strict sense of right and wrong. His trust, or approval, or love, once lost was lost forever. However, academic achievements impress him, as do careers, which carry status, so that would get his attention and approval and 'love' every time.

So Ellie grew up developing a Caretaker Personality. She is in many ways like her mum, in that she is always there for everyone, will never say no to anyone needing help, champions every cause going - especially any to do with the rights of children or vulnerable adults - and is tireless in her giving of herself and her time. She is exhausted and emotionally drained a great deal of the time, spreads herself extremely thinly, and deep down is extremely angry. However, she tries very hard to put that away, and sublimates it by doing more and more good works, which helps to take some of the guilt away, at least.

So let's look at what Ellie has learned to believe about life:

+ You are loved for what you do, not for who you are.
+ Other people judge you by what you give them and do for them, and by what status you achieve.
+ You mustn't ever mind doing things for people, and you mustn't ever mind if you do not get much thanks. Helping is what life is all about, and it is what gets you loved.

+ There are rights and wrongs in life, things are black and white, and there are no greys. Especially where other people's views of you are concerned. One wrong move, one *no* said to someone, means the loss of love or approval for evermore.

+ People are fragile. If you upset them, they will not be able to get over it. If you hurt them, the wound will go so deep it can never be healed. If you trouble them with your problems or worries, they will not be able to sleep or rest and you will have spoiled their peace of mind. Therefore, you must learn to just deal with things on your own. Even big things.

So back to the therapist in my pocket:

+ The Caretaker Personality has never known unconditional love, but has learned to believe that you earn love by what you do. This love can be lost at any moment, and nothing you ever do will be enough.

+ Your needs are too big, too much, and they are bad, they are selfish, they are ugly, they are shameful. No one must see them, and the moment you get 'needy' or cross or unhappy or 'grumpy' the thing to do is get busy. It is the way to deal with feelings because talking and sharing has never been ok.

Recognize any of that? Then you need to know that *none of it is true*. I know it *seems* true but it is *not* true. Unconditional love *does* exist, people *can* love you just for being you, and you don't *have* to save the world, and you don't *have* to take care of other people's worry tendencies, because that is *their* responsibility. Not yours. And your parents were *human*. They did the best they could, with the resources they had, but they were/are on their journey just as you are on yours, and it is not your job to hold that up by protecting them from themselves and their own light bulb moments. In fact, it is *none of your business*!

Can you feel the relief of that? It is *none* of your business, *none* of it. Let it all go, move on. Free yourself. Accept yourself just the way you are. And then you can start really living!

Sacred dance

We are forever giving
to each other
the precious gift of a mirror,
and then moving on.
So many seemingly small encounters,
but each one significant.
And, through that gift,
we are profoundly changed.
Each of us is changed
and takes that change
out into the world.
For nothing is accidental;
We are dancing
the sacred dance of Life

Our stories

· ·

Our lives are made up of a series of stories. Have you noticed? We love creating stories; we write the story of our life in them and through them. We love writing them and telling them. If you allow yourself to ponder this awhile, you will discover that it is impossible not to think in terms of stories. You cannot have a thought without turning it into a story. You cannot have an experience, however brief, without writing a story about it in your mind. It is how we give meaning to seemingly random happenings in our lives. It is how we link everything together and join everything up.

Our whole life becomes a story. However, sometimes, we can find ourselves liking our story so much that we cease to remember the way it really was. We tell that story to ourselves, and to others, over and over until it becomes true. What started out as just a story becomes filled out so that in our memory it now becomes absolute. We refine it so well, and we discard everything that conflicts with our 'story' and emphasize everything that supports it, that, in the end the story we tell IS our story. We like this way of organizing experience neatly so much that we become very good storytellers. Our stories become bigger, grander, and more rigidly defined every single time we tell them. And it rarely occurs to us that we are excluding huge chunks of our experience by allowing this to happen.

And that is okay. Nothing is ever not okay. Everything is the most wonderfully delicious opportunity for learning and expansion. It is part of what we are here to do. To grow and expand. It is part of what makes living fun.

And our stories are valuable, significant, important, uniquely ours. These experiences happened to us, and they deserve to be told. Need to be told. They are our version of an experience that has many versions. As many versions as there are possibilities. But let's also feed in here who we really are, and why our stories, the writing of them, the giving meaning to them, the creation of metaphor though them, the view of life we develop in the telling of them, are so utterly central, vital, to the ebb and flow of the life we came here to experience. We came here *in order* to write a story. A completely new and unique, never before told and never to be told again story. We came here to go through the struggle of creating meaning and finding something new in the process of discovering that meaning. We came here to grow by becoming a storyteller. To turn our experiences into a story through becoming an observer of our experience as well as living it as the experiencer. To be a witnesser.

And *that* is the thing. That is the crucial bit. It is a funny old process, this business of choosing to incarnate in the service of expansion. It is meant to be fun. Even the bits that perhaps don't feel so great at the time. We always come out the other side, and when we do, we have another story to tell, another golden nugget of learning and wisdom. And we weave this new story into all the other stories we have already written, and by doing so add a new dimension, something more that was not there before. Are you coming to appreciate how complex this storytelling we do really is?

So when you are writing a story, make sure to remember that it is a draft only, and not the polished, finished article. Never forget that you will never ever complete it. That it will never ever be done. And that it is always and forever being edited and re-worked. And also, never lose sight of the fact that your story in any given moment is biased. That it is limited. That it is based on carefully sifted and specifically chosen data. That someone else telling your story may well not tell it the same way. That on a different day, even you might not tell it the same way. Or that you, with the benefit of more information than you had available at the time when you first wrote this particular version of your story, might well make your story far more complex than you originally did. Put in other perspectives, other characters, and other information. You might fill in some of the gaps.

You see, if we do not do that - recognize that we are only writing a draft and not the final story - we limit ourselves. We shut down the wonderful gift of expansion of this lifetime. We cease to allow ourselves to keep changing and flowing, refining, integrating, and growing. Instead, we stay on safe ground and simply tell the same old story over and over again. We tell it so many times that we know it by heart. We become so familiar with the way we tell it that we no longer stop to question whether or not it is still accurate or how embellished or lop-sided it may have become. Memory is a funny old thing if we do not keep reminding ourselves that it is always work in progress.

The story we so often end up telling contains a fair proportion of fiction along with the parts that are true. Do you know just how subjective our perception and our memory recall is, once we embrace this brief experiment of a life in this time/space reality? How colored by how it was on the day? By our subconscious motives, wishes, fears? By other memories? By the way, we want things to look and sound to others? By shame? By guilt? And do you begin to get just how glorious that is? What a magical and profound piece of manifesting that is? Are you in awe yet?

We really do create our own truth. We are living life the ego's way, just as we came here to do. We are not doing anything pathological or wrong here. It is not a problem that we do this. It actually means that everything is absolutely on track. We are doing very successfully, what we came here to do: we are creating the illusion of a specific and particular personal reality in order that our chosen drama can play out. That is the beauty of this wonderful partnership of ego and amnesia that we, as Source energy, have manifested so thoroughly and so successfully.

And so here's the next level, the crux of it: by creating our very own truth, our own version of reality, by building an ego which will be selective in its recall, the themes we have chosen to play out in this lifetime in order for

Source to expand become drawn. It is all on course. It is how it is meant to happen. Hold that thought while I tell you about Susie.

Susie is a woman in her mid-forties, and she has an extremely powerful story going on. You may find some of it familiar. You may find that bits of her story resonate with bits of your own, here and there.

Susie's story tells how, every time she starts to allow herself to feel something for a man, the man changes from being kind and loving into someone who treats her mockingly, unkindly. From someone who wants her to someone who is pushing her away again and again. Susie tells everyone that this is the story of her life. All her girlfriends know this and commiserate with her. It is a much told and much explored story. And it never changes. And it always turns out to be right. However, if we were to watch a while, listen some, tune in to what is going on, we would begin to see that Susie is not neutral in all this.

Susie is actually setting this up over and over again. She would be very cross, affronted, defensive, if you tried to suggest such a thing. However, the longer you watched, the more obvious it would become.

You would see an eager, attractive, outgoing woman, one who had no trouble forming romantic relationships. You would watch the romance unfold, and think that all was going well. But then you would see a tipping point, you would notice the change. You would see this woman become wary, cautious, troubled, doubting. You would have to look carefully or you would miss it. Nevertheless, suddenly this woman would be testing. She would be doing lots of little things designed to see if this man really did love her, if he would stay, or if he would be like 'all the others'. And by so doing, she would be ensuring that this story would go the way of all the others. Because we all know about law of attraction. Don't we?

When I was a newbie psychotherapist in training, many years ago now, we learned about Freud's 'Compulsion to Repeat.' This man had observed that we return again and again to a point of pain until we somehow manage to resolve it. And that this point of pain is almost always created in our childhood. He knew what he was talking about, did Freud. He got lots right. However, he was also a man of his time, and so his thinking was limited to that time. From Freud we get a medical model, not a spiritual model. He did not have the benefit of the knowledge we now have about energy and vibration, law of attraction, leading edge spirituality. But he certainly set us off on the right track. He knew about the ego and the conscious and unconscious mind. He recognized defenses, and so much of what he observed and formulated, way back then, holds true today. We just need to put a slightly different slant on it. I would like to offer that different slant, if I may, for you to consider.

I would like to suggest that the ego, that part of us which is so often maligned by spiritual thinkers and teachers right now, has a spiritual purpose. In addition, I would like to suggest that it is related to the amnesia we experience when we enter this physical time/place reality. I would like to suggest, after many years of observing it, firstly as a psychotherapist, and now as an awakening woman who still has a therapist in her pocket, that the ego is the character we have chosen, which will play out the role we have chosen, which will give rise to the themes we have chosen, which will lead to the expansion we have chosen, for this lifetime we have chosen. And that it is through the stories that will evolve through the living of this role, mine and yours and everyone else's, that Source is forever expanding.

Let me say that again. The ego is the character we have chosen, which will play out the role we have chosen, which will give rise to the themes we have chosen, which will lead to the expansion we have chosen, for this lifetime we have chosen. Throughout this entire process, we remain the powerful creator we actually are. And the limits we impose, initially, upon our knowledge of who we really are, and why we really came, are voluntary and self-imposed. So we employ the ego in the service of expansion. As creators. And we have chosen it all. And we write the story of it in our way, through our eyes, as part of that amazing process.

Therefore, back to Susie. And her story of being rejected again and again.

Let's look at Susie's childhood for a moment. Susie's father was a man who was emotionally pretty shut down. (By the way, he too is Source energy playing out a role. He has adopted this set of characteristics, just as Susie has adopted hers, for the purpose of the themes of this lifetime only. His ego has been the vehicle for that, just as Susie's has. This is not who either of them actually are). Nevertheless, Susie's relationship with her father has been unsatisfactory, full of a mix of painful longing and the shame of rejection. This relationship has set the scene. And now the drama is ready to unfold. That is the challenge, and the adventure, of this lifetime.

Susie's ego, her set of characteristics, her receptacle for the fears and pain she will either resolve during this lifetime or expand in the process of trying to resolve, has been built through the multitude of experiences she has gone through from the moment her soul entered her body. The ego acts as the catalyst for her chosen 'drama' and is the force behind the working out of her story. Therefore, what we are writing as our story is always subjective. And that in no way invalidates it. It merely means we need to keep reviewing and rewriting it. Because it is *always* subjective. That is the challenge and the learning. That is what expansion comes out of. The reworking of our stories. Both individually and with others. That is the true purpose of the story. Not the story itself.

It is how Source, the energy of love and light that we all are, expands. Expansion always comes via contrast. Through the stories we create, and then live out. We are weaving the most intricate web of interconnecting and interactive experience, emotionally and psychologically driven, through which our higher self, our source, grows in wisdom, compassion, unconditional love, strength and power. This playground is serving many layers of purpose at once. And we are creating it.

Law of attraction, therefore, and the understanding of energy and vibration, is not some separate device that we must learn to incorporate in our thinking and awareness and day-to-day life. To see it that way is to still believe the illusion of separateness. To fail to see that we do not *use* law of attraction; we *are* law of attraction. We are the creators of our reality. But of *all* our reality. Not just the 'good' bits. When you see it like this, when you realize that you are at no point a victim of life's circumstances, but rather the creator of them; and you understand how central your work as a storyteller is; and when you can see beyond your limited and human view of how your life *ought* to be, and can see instead that you are Source *choosing* these life experiences for the purpose of expansion, then everything falls into place and you stop needing to resist or fight your current reality. You know it is a story, and that you are writing it.

So now back to the ego: the ego is not really our enemy. It is the bit of us that willingly tolerates amnesia for the purpose of facilitating expansion. Once we know that, we can view things in a very different light. If we are Susie, for example, we can start to notice the situations and experiences our ego places us in over and over again. We can begin to see the themes running through these situations, and become the observer of the story that is unfolding, and not just the central character. We can begin to see that we create by attracting the conditions that are ripe for this unfolding. That it is always exactly as it needs to be. Always. We can remember how powerful we really are. That we are choosing. That the story that is unfolding is the story we are writing, and that we are in charge.

And as we learn this fundamental truth, we find ourselves becoming liberated. We come to recognize that we are not our story, and that our story is not who we are. We are, in fact, the editor, gathering information and making sure all the angles are covered. An editor with an objective interest in getting to the truth, not in just spinning a yarn. And when we can consistently question, refine, rework, redraft, rethink, we have developed the capacity to mentalize (understand that others' psyches and received experience differs from our own), to empathize, to accept and allow rather than judge. To stand back and watch and observe and choose, and choose again, and to consciously manifest all we want to manifest. Because once we have reached that point, the expansion has already happened, we have remembered, we are once again conscious creators of our reality. The amnesia has gone.

We begin to act from our source, our essence, rather than from the ego. The ego tells stories; our source observes and experiences. The ego defends one version of the story; our source sees infinite variations. The ego needs to show; our source simply sees. Without judgment or investment in a particular version. Simply with love and compassion for the oneness we all are. See, that is the true value of your story. It never was about you, not really. Because it was never about the you that you believed yourself to be when you wrote those first simplistic egocentric stories. It was about you at the leading edge, source energy expanding, always and forever.

It was always about the you that is this radiant pure light energy, of immense power and wisdom and strength and gentleness, just writing a story. And when you look back at all that has happened, all you have experienced and survived, tasted and learned, you will be *amazed*. And the cheers and the applause, the appreciation and the joy, will fill the universe. That is how important and significant you are. *You*. Not the story that you have made up. *You*. You are the dreamer of dreams and the spinner of the web. You create, and then you observe, your creation. Don't you find that truly awesome!

Namaste

Who were you,
seeming stranger,
young angry man
with hatred and hurt
in your eyes?
When you glanced at me,
a split second
only,
but there was more than
a lifetime in that look.
I felt it, and know you did too.
You were startled,
because your hate
was met by warmth,
and you were bemused,
thrown by kindness.
In that moment
our lives intertwined,
and we were both aware
and open.
I saw the fragility
in the nonchalant glance
meant to wound,
the burning, the yearning
for recognition.
The hurt and the tears
held at bay

by the anger.
And you saw - what?
Something that startled you,
that, for sure.
A triggered remembering,
a fleeting knowing,
a seeing, an invitation, maybe.
It was one of those
meant to happen moments,
a tiny thread
we were both meant to weave
in the oh so brief
encounter we had planned
back then, before.
A blessing, a lesson,
a mirror, a reflection,
all of these?
This evening you are
in my mind,
just as I know
I will be in yours.
Our souls touched
and spoke to each other today.
We are both
forever changed.
Thank you. My friend.

On Compassion

Very early on in training, I came up against the issue of how to work with shame. I felt so conflicted about how to help, while worrying about how not to do damage by my potential clumsiness, that I took the situation to supervision.

I had begun seeing a client, a young man, who had known dreadful humiliation, as a result of having been violently raped as a boy, and who felt the shame of it so badly, even now, that he struggled to speak of how awful those experiences had been with me. Yet he clearly wanted so badly to find some relief, and was here in my therapy room, asking me to meet him where he was. He was haunted and wanted to be free.

I did not want to invade or intrude, or cause further shame, but neither did I want to leave him feeling alone or isolated. To make him feel 'other' or 'over there.' Equally, I could see just how appallingly painful it was to come and ask for help, and just how exposing it felt to try to talk about what had happened. I also knew, because it was impossible not to know, that until this young man had found comfort and release by sharing his shame and the pain of it, and seeing it accepted fully by another, there could be no such relief. What my supervisor offered me was a profoundly wise and compassionate observation. It was not about him at all; it was about me. Supervisors are canny that way.

She asked me why I was so afraid of the pain. At first, I looked at her a bit blankly, puzzled. But she asked me again, very gently. To my horror, I found that I had tears welling up in my eyes. However, something had also melted inside me.

I had realised, in that moment, that to go near to this young man's shame would mean going close to my own. It was not just about making him feel exposed, it was that I dreaded how exposed I might also feel, how painful going near to pain is. But how much more difficult, very specifically, going near to shame would be. Most of us find it incredibly hard if someone lays themselves bear by sharing with us how shaming something was, or tells us just how ashamed, in painful detail, they are of something they have discovered in themselves. I was certainly finding it hard at this point in my early training. Every part of me wanted to run.

We human beings tend to adopt a number of different strategies to try to avoid going too close. Our intentions are good, but *every single one leaves the other person isolated and shamed further:*

So, we minimise what happened, say it was nothing, tell the person that others have revealed far worse things about themselves, and let others see much more awful things than this. We say they should just let it go, not think about it anymore. Without realising it, by doing so we simply leave the other totally alone and feeling unheard. Or we tell a story intended to illustrate that we have said, done, experienced, revealed something just like it, or even worse. We believe that by showing that we are even worse than they are, we will remove the other's shame. However, all this achieves is to make it about us. It reveals the device we are employing to try to distance ourselves from their own situation. Shame recognises that straight away. It is so tuned in to the attempt to avoid that it seeks it straight away. So, again, the person asking to be understood and to find relief is left alone in their own burning sense of humiliation at having dared to ask.

Alternatively, we confirm, by being overcome ourselves by the degree of the other person's shame, and by not being able to separate ourselves from it sufficiently to be of help, that it is truly an awful thing that has happened. That is, we offer sympathy instead of empathy - the classic 'poor you' grenade that people at a loss for what to say can throw. In doing this, we place a divide between the other and ourselves. We convey that we are looking on, appalled, unable to see them because all we can see is ourselves and how we would be suffering if we were them. Or, in our shock, we can imply criticism or blame, through being simply incredulous and letting our mouth drop wide open in amazement. There is no good way of recovering from this. The damage is done and no more sharing can be done. We have confirmed the other's worse fears: that this thing they want to try to speak about truly *is* unspeakable, and they were wrong to risk trying to speak it.

And so when my supervisor asked me why I was so afraid of the pain, I knew that she had seen my own vulnerability, my own capacity to feel shame, and how afraid I was of being placed in danger of having it opened up by allowing myself to be vulnerable to the experience of shame in another. To the pain of it. To the sleepless night to follow of it.

Most of us fear pain. Physical pain, though hard, is often easier for is to face than emotional or psychological pain. Going near *that* pain challenges us, opens us up, and tears us apart, far more searingly than does physical pain. And yet, I have learned over the years that, if we can go into such pain rather than closing it off or running away from it, the healing and relief is immense. As is the growth in our compassion. I would even say that the depth of our compassion is directly proportionate to the extent of our healed shame. There is nothing quite so powerful for encouraging our unconditional acceptance of the flaws we perceive in others as having forgiven our own. And the love that we are able to give out to the world is directly proportionate to the amount of unconditional love that we are able to feel for ourselves.

It is only by being willing to expose ourselves to our own vulnerability that we can meet another where they are in their own vulnerability. There is no other way. To offer anything less is to confirm to the other that we want nothing to do with it, that we are separate from it and looking on from a distance, unwilling to share their pain.

Now, I fully realise that this territory I am laying out is fraught with difficulty. I do not mean to ignore the fact that there are some people who are looking for someone not to share their pain with, but to *give* it to. The people who want to simply dump it somewhere else, and walk away lightened while they leave you dripping with it all. Or the people who want to tell it over and over again to as many people who will listen, but who never move on from it because it has become a way of life for them, and their identity.

I am not talking about those people, the ones who cannot yet take responsibility for their own feelings and experience. I am talking about someone who is taking responsibility, who is aware, who is doing the thinking and the feeling and the work, and who simply needs to tell someone else, now, at this point, in order to complete this particular journey of painful self-discovery and, ultimately, liberation. And I am suggesting that, if we are the one who is given this gift to hold, if we are the soul and fellow traveller they happen, with care and thought, to choose, then we are going to find ourselves up against our own fear of vulnerability and pain. And so I would like to offer a thought about that. It is what helped me in that moment of realisation in my supervisor's room. And the truth of it has stayed with me, and grown, ever since.

It is that we are not *separate*. Simply, that we are *not separate*.

Now, these are very easy words to say. We may understand the concept, the theory. We read the words, we devour the books, we listen to the enlightened speakers, we hold the spiritually aware conversations, and we can talk the talk. But how about the bit that is about walking the walk? What then? What about the bit that says, everything you are, I am also? Or, everything you have known, I too know? Or, everything I see in you is also right here, in me? How about the bit that says, and *knows*, truly *knows*, we are the same, we are one, everything I feel you also are feeling, and everything you are experiencing I, too, am going through and growing through? How about the bit that says there is no difference between you and me? None. For when I look on, I am seeing simply another part of myself. Therefore, your pain is my pain; your shame is my shame. Why would I hide from the gift? Your relief is my relief. Your liberation is my liberation. We are walking together, fellow souls on a journey of expansion, and there is no difference between us other than the form we have chosen to take in this current lifetime. What about that bit?

When we really get that, and when we integrate it into our being so thoroughly that we live it, everyone becomes free and we need no longer hide from each other. Every encounter becomes a gift, every sharing a deepening of our common humanity and common divinity. We appreciate, rather than judge. We go towards rather than away from. We reach out rather than pulling back.

And then, even those who are not yet where we are, but one day will be, those who are looking still to place responsibility elsewhere, to dump and move on, become a gift, since in our very recognition of what they are wanting to do, and our understanding of why they are wanting to do it, we expand our own compassion in the remembering that there was a time when we were in that place too. And we see, all over again, the oneness of all that is, and the perfection of the imperfection we all come here to be. And shame is at the heart of that, since there is nothing quite like shame for throwing into sharp and poignant focus the beauty of who we really are. Or for helping us to learn what we came here to learn.

And there is nothing that is quite like the compassion that comes to us, as a flood of profound recognition and humility, when we truly understand that.

Danny

· ·

Time for another fairy tale...

This one is about a little boy called Danny. It could so easily be about a little boy called Sam or Edward, or a little girl called Sarah or Katie. However, in our story, just now, it is a little boy called Danny.

Are you sitting comfortably? Then I will begin...

There was once a little boy called Danny. He was a very lucky and much loved little boy who, from the moment he was born, received nothing but praise. And we all know how very important it is to receive praise. Danny was praised for being such a good baby, who slept through the night very quickly. He was praised for never being too demanding, and his mummy would tell all her friends how, if he would have a temper tantrum - at least, that's what she called it - when he woke in the night, having not long been fed, or was a little bit damp, she could just ignore him for a while and he would stop crying and let her go back to sleep.

Danny's mummy badly wanted a good baby, because she had been quite worried about how she might cope if he needed her too much. Danny's mummy had a great need for peace and quiet, and for things to be predictable and steady, so she had been quite worried in case having a baby might shake things up too much. As Danny grew into a toddler, he could not help noticing that there were days when his mummy cried a lot, and others when she seemed very sad. Sometimes, his daddy, who wasn't there a lot of the time, would come home and shout a lot, and make his mummy cry some more. There was a lot of sadness.

Danny started to try to work out how he could protect his mummy and look after her. He needed her to be ok, because she was his safety, and so he began to realize, in a simple sort of way, that it was his job to make sure that she was happy.

So Danny taught himself how to be extremely patient, very considerate, and to never make a fuss. Even when he felt like making a fuss, because he felt cross or upset or something did not seem fair. It did not matter if he was not feeling fine, just as long as his mummy was not sad or crying. Danny became very good at this. He learned how to notice when his mummy needed a hug, or a tissue, or a biscuit, or to borrow his teddy. And he also learned to behave very carefully when his daddy was home, so that he would not make things any worse by causing an argument or by making his daddy shout. Danny knew by now, so clearly, that his job was to keep things safe, and to keep everybody happy. He didn't know any more whether he himself was happy or sad, cross or frightened, worried or upset. He had stopped noticing that a long time ago. But he *was* extremely good at doing this most important - indeed, vital - job of keeping everyone else happy.

When Danny got to school, he also impressed the teachers with how patient and kind and protective he was. He always seemed to know what was the right thing to do at any given moment. He would notice when other children were sad, and would spend his break times keeping them company, walking around the playground with them, arm around their shoulders. When Danny's mummy and daddy would go to parents' evenings, they would come away glowing with pride at all they were being told about their little boy. They learned that he was a monitor for this, and a monitor for that. They learned that he had even organized a litter patrol in his break times, when he would go round picking up all the litter in the playground that other children had dropped. He got a special award for that. The teacher even said - and this made his mummy and daddy exceptionally proud - that he was *so* well behaved in class that often, if you didn't actually look up and see him there, sitting right at the back quietly getting on with his work without a fuss, you could *even* forget that he was there at all. Danny's mummy and daddy thought this was just wonderful, and congratulated each other on what a successful job they had done of bringing him up.

There was a tiny rocky patch when Danny hit his teens. He went through a stage of liking certain things that his parents didn't approve of, wanting to wear clothes his parents didn't approve of, listening to music his parents didn't approve of, and wanting to hang out with friends in a way that his parents didn't approve of. He tried hard in his way to do these things, but one day his mum said something that frightened him to his core. She said, ' After all I've done for you, you treat me like this! I can't stand the sight of you. You've broken my heart. Go away, I can't bear to be around you.'

And finally, Danny realized the truth of things.

He realized that if you want people to love you, to approve of you and want to be around you, you must always do what they want you to do, and be what they want you to be. The fear of it being any other way, of losing his mother and father's love and approval, was so great, and was so paralyzing, that in that moment the course of the rest of his life felt like it was set. He sat on the floor in his bedroom, in the dark, and pondered the most important truth of his young life.

Then, one day, Danny looked at himself in the mirror and could see, by the way his body had changed, that he had become a grown up. He did not feel any different inside, but it was clear from his body that he had, indeed, grown up. He realized that he was now expected to go out into the world, get a good job, find himself a girlfriend, buy a house, settle down, have a family, save for his old age, and live his life patiently and contentedly, and not want anything for himself or make a fuss. He tried very hard to do this, because he wanted to make his parents really proud. Especially since he had caused them so much stress and in his teens.

But then something terrible started to happen. Something really terrible. He had never experienced anything like it in his life before. He found that he started to feel really angry inside. Explosively angry. Utter rage. And worse still, he found that this explosive rage would leak out suddenly when he was not expecting it. With his girlfriend, with his work colleagues, with total strangers in the street, or people serving at counters, or in cafes. And it was not a straightforward, clean sort of anger. It was nasty, mocking, and sarcastic. He found that he sometimes just wanted to hurt. He knew it was cruel, that the words once out of his mouth could never be unsaid. But he was terrified to discover that he simply did not care! He was not safe anywhere. He was a really bad person. Such a bad person. How had it come to this?

Suddenly, he found himself running. Running from it all. From the nastiness, from the hurt, from the confusion. From the mess. Most of all, from the mess. And then, as he ran, he found the roadway turning into a path, and then the path into a grassy track, the ground suddenly soft under his feet instead of hard and jarring. The air smelt different. Cleaner, lighter, like suddenly he could breathe. He bent over, doubled up, catching his breath in huge, deep gasps. It felt like he had been running for miles and miles. He wanted to stop. Just to stop. For it *all* to stop!

From bending double, gasping for air, he sank down, knees bent, and knelt on the ground. He found himself looking round. He had no idea how he had arrived at this place, but he seemed to be in a forest. He could smell the richness of the slightly damp ground he was kneeling on, and realized he found it surprisingly soothing, refreshing, and comforting. Sunlight found its way here and there down to the forest floor from high up in the canopy, and in one spot, where the sun threw down a full beam onto an outcrop of rocks, he noticed an old woman.

She did not appear to be aware of him at first. She was weaving something in her hands, and seemed totally absorbed. However, he realized that he also knew, somehow and somewhere deep down inside, that this woman knew he was there with every fiber of her being. She was just waiting. He rather liked this feeling; it was new. No one had ever waited for him like this before. They had always been expecting, never waiting. He cleared his throat. It was the way he had learned to attract attention without making too much of a fuss. It was being polite. To his surprise, the old woman appeared not to notice. She just carried on weaving whatever she was weaving with those nimble fingers of hers.

Danny found himself with a dilemma. Should he clear his throat again? Should he just wait? Should he just tiptoe quietly away? He decided he would clear his throat again. A little louder this time. Not too loud, just a little. He felt a strange pull to this old woman, though he had no idea why. He just knew he was meant to be here, in this place, at this moment, and that she had known he was coming and had been waiting for him.

The old woman clearly registered the second throat clearing. She inclined her head slightly towards him, as if acknowledging the sound, but still made no attempt to speak. She was listening though. Most definitely really listening. She was aware of everything that was going on, outside of him, but also inside. Then she startled him. She laid whatever she was weaving down on the ground. And then slowly, purposefully, she lifted her head and looked straight at him. She had the most amazing eyes. They were dark, deep pools of fluid wisdom and knowing. She *knew*, and even though she knew, it was *okay*.

He could not get his head around that one. Even though she knew, it was still ok. Those dark, deep pools held his, and he found himself letting go. Oh of so much. The eyes saw and absorbed and waited. Suddenly, it felt a bit uncomfortable, like the shared gaze had gone on for just a tiny bit too long, and he broke it to look at the ground and to stroke his hand across the grass and moss where he was still kneeling.

The old woman spoke. 'My child,' she said. It was a voice both gentle and strong, quite compelling. He did not know why she had called him that. As far as he was aware, they had never met before. 'Who are you?' he asked. 'My child.' Again, those strange words. They made no sense... and yet, they did. 'What have you come back for?' It was getting really weird now. What was this about coming back? He had not been away. Had he? 'What do you mean?' Danny asked. He was both intrigued and nervous. He wanted to understand. Why had he come back? Why? The old woman looked at him again. Her gaze was steady, unwavering, and kindly. She could see so much more than he could, and yet she was waiting for him to know it. What *had* he come back for? *What?*

Then, he knew. Suddenly, he *knew*. Oh, the realization was so very wonderful. He could hardly contain his laughter. And then, all in a rush, he could not contain it. It exploded out of him, just like so much anger and rage had exploded out of him for months and months. And once he had started, he found he could not stop. The laughter burst out of him. Loud, hysterical laughter, as if he had just heard the funniest joke of his entire life. At first, it was a man's laughter, loud and deep, then it became a belly laugh, then a boy's giggles and eventually it had become the most joyous peel of laughter he had ever heard. And astonishingly, it was coming out of him!

The old woman's eyes were merry, twinkling, encouraging. She smiled the most wonderful smile, and grinned as he laughed and laughed. And my goodness, how he laughed. He could suddenly see it all, and could feel a lightness as it all lifted from his shoulders. The weight of a lifetime. 'It never *was* my job, was it?' He finally managed to speak, and his voice was steadier. 'All that...stuff...it was never my job.' 'No wonder you were angry, my child. You have taken so much on yourself that was never yours to have to take. And you have lost your joy.' And then softly, almost in a whisper, ' And that, as you have now realized, is what you came back for.' She smiled, and held his gaze again, raising her eyebrows as she saw his recognition, saw it all sinking in and fitting into place, and nodded gently.

'And now,' the old woman said, in a tone that said they were both ready, 'there is fun to be had and adventures to go on! So you'd better go back so you don't miss them!' Then, such a magical chuckle, like a thousand tinkling bells, and the old woman threw her hands up in the air and laughed and laughed. When she finally stopped, Danny was standing in front of her, holding out his arms. He had no idea whether or not this was ok, but he rather sensed that she would know that this was the most spontaneous thing he had ever done in his life. And that she would not shame him.

The old woman's face melted into the most radiant, beaming smile, and she stood up and held her arms wide open. And when he sank into those arms, into the most complete and satisfying embrace he had ever known, he felt a strange remembering, of a place he had known before, of being held like this before, of being known and loved so unconditionally, just like this, before. *He remembered!*

It was the old woman who broke the embrace and, with tears in her eyes, stroked his cheek, and planted a kiss there. 'And now,' she smiled, 'it really is time.' The air all around shimmered with a strange light and, before his eyes, Danny watched as the old woman whose embrace he had just felt so tangibly seemed to become a thousand sparkling fireflies, and merge into the brightness that now lit up the entire clearing. 'Until next time!' the tinkling voice laughed. 'Be sure to have lots of adventures! I'll be always sharing the fun!'

And that is exactly what Danny did.

The embrace

. . . .

There is an embrace
so complete
so secure
and yet so free
which holds
all things
in its gentle,
tender awareness.
An energy
of Love and Light
of unimaginable power.
It is holding
you now
and now
and now

Little girl on a climbing frame

The other day, as I sat in a pub garden one evening enjoying the sunshine, I watched a tiny drama being acted out. You could easily have missed it. It lasted all of thirty seconds. However, in that thirty seconds something huge happened in a little girl's life. The little girl in question was playing on a wooden climbing frame, consisting of a castle, turret, and slide. Her daddy was standing at the bottom of the ladder you had to climb up to get onto it, and she was playing a delicious game.

She would run up the little runway to the turret at the top, then turn and run joyously back down towards her daddy, laughing openly and freely in the anticipation that when she reached him he would blow her a huge kiss and laugh back. They were playing a game that told her that, in that moment, she was the center of his world, and it felt wonderful.

Then the tiny drama occurred. While she was running up towards the turret, with her back to him, her daddy was called over to sort out something to do with a food order, and another daddy moved into that space and helped his little son up the ladder. The little girl ran down excitedly, squealing with laughter, to the place where she expected her daddy to be, full of anticipation once again of the blown kiss and the intimacy between them. But instead, she pulled up short as she ran face to face into this other man, a stranger. Her confusion was tangible, and she clearly did not know what to do. Then she did what she had learned to do with her daddy when he was not really paying her attention.

She put her head on one side and smiled widely at the man.

But instead of responding with a smile back, like she had expected, this man looked right through her, as if she did not exist, and then shouted at his son who was crawling on his hands and knees up the slope and getting dirty. In that split second, the drama occurred.

You could so easily have missed it. And if you had seen it, you might not have thought that anything of significance had happened. But I registered the change in this little girl's face, the lowering of her eyes, the slump of her shoulders, the thumb suddenly going into her mouth for comfort. The *shame*. She sidled off, and sat down in a corner of the climbing frame, clearly troubled and confused.

Now that was just a tiny, almost imperceptible drama, and her daddy quickly noticed where she was and, although he didn't know what had caused her change of mood, he responded by sweeping her up in his arms and blowing into her neck, making her giggle and wriggle, and everything was restored. But here's the thing. Supposing that this tiny drama were to happen every single day, many times a day. And that the man (or woman) who looked straight through her was not a stranger, but her mummy or daddy. Then time and again that little girl would experience the shame of openly anticipating and hoping and opening up, only to feel the shame of having got it wrong, of having misjudged it, having expected too much, discovering she was *not worthy*.

Because this is the root of all shame. It is the sense that we hoped for something that we clearly didn't deserve, opened ourselves up and revealed what we hoped for or were anticipating, only to discover it was not reciprocated; dared to think we deserved something only to realize painfully that we were not considered worthy of it. Shame is always about humiliation resulting from a mismatch of expectations. Those awful comments adults make to children, about being 'too big for their boots,' or questions like, 'What makes you think you're so special?' do exactly this to a child. And the damage is seen years later, in grown up children who feel unworthy, unlovable, confused about intimacy, ashamed of being open or showing love. And then the damage goes down through another generation, and another.

A wonderful analyst, writing years ago, a man by the name of Kohut, was one of my absolute heroes when I was training as a therapist. He stated, quite simply, that in order to give a child a sense of worthiness and their place in the world, the child needed to feel and experience that they were 'the sparkle in their mother's eye.' For 'mother', you could just as easily substitute 'father'. Or 'significant carer.' And another wonderful theorist, Donald Winnicott, talked about the need a child has to see themselves first in the mirror of their parent's eyes before they can have a sense of existing fully in their own right.

We learned, as therapists in the making, that the relationship that a client formed with us was a 'second chance.' That is, that the therapist could mirror back to the client that they were seen, understood, and known, and that the client could experience being allowed to sparkle, and to be the sparkle in the therapist's eyes for a while. I have seen the power of relationship, and of being truly seen, heal so much, and I know the power of that mirror that we can hold up for each other.

Let each us be that mirror, each and every one of us, and let us never for a moment underestimate the wonderful gift we bestow on each other in the offering of one of the greatest experiences any of us can ever have: that it is fine, and not shameful to seek and to give love, and that we are more than worthy to do so.

Love said to me

Love said to me,
Let me in,
and I told Love
I was afraid,
and said, I do not
know who you are.
Love replied,
Do you not
recognise me?
Yet? Still?
And I looked
again,
into eyes which
were a mirror
of my own.
Come in,
my dearest,
oldest friend,
I whispered.
You have been
gone
too long

The real magic

I am sitting in a motorway services sipping a coffee, my mind taken up with where I have been and where I am going, when I am suddenly captivated by a family sitting a little way in front of me. Specifically, by the baby who is bouncing up and down gleefully, laughing and grinning and happy, on his mother's knee as she hold him upright in a standing position so he can flex his legs and discover what they can do In this moment, both for mother and baby, there is nothing else. They are totally absorbed in what is happening between them, and the sheer joy and fun of it. The loving bond is tangible; I can feel it even at a distance. I can also see something else, and it is quite magical. It is this:

This baby does not yet know that he is separate. For this baby, his mother is a part of him and he is a part of her; they are one and the same being. You can see this by the way he interacts with her. He treats her body as if it is an extension of his, when she laughs he clearly experiences it as if it is him laughing, he knows they are in complete unison. There is as yet no 'other. As I watch this baby, I realize that he is barely here yet. He is only very newly arrived in this big earth playground. He is wide eyed and full of the energy from which he has have come. In his perception of the world, he is still barely physical. He still knows he is source energy; he still remembers.

He is pure light energy, still shimmering and settling into his body, still in touch with the heartbeat from which he has come. He is full of the freedom to be. He as yet knows no other way than to be fully and gloriously himself. He is also a very powerful creator, who manifests exactly what he wants with ease. He wants something to happen, he puts it out there, and he experiences instant manifestation. He never doubts for a moment that what he is wanting, through feeling and imagining, will come to him. And so it does. He is insistent, confident and clear, and knows that he is worthy.

It is that quality in babies we so enjoy about babies, isn't it? It is part of what makes them so loveable. This baby is still free to be the unconditional love that he actually is. He has not yet clothed himself in the vast layers of disguise and defense with which we, who have been here so much longer, have learned to clothe ourselves. He has not yet learned the ways of the world. He is not wearing a mask; he has not yet learned how to pretend. He is not putting a particular face on for the world. What you see, when you look into his face, and when you watch with delight as he embraces fully the experience he is currently caught up in, is his true nature. He is real in ways that we have ceased to know how to be real. He has not yet learned to be any other way. It is clear, watching, that this world he has recently jumped into is fascinating and exciting and that he is unashamedly curious and unapologetically open and honest in his experiencing of it. He is still anticipating life as the great adventure that he set out upon when he decided to come. He still perceives abundance surrounding him.

However, it is the recognition that he does not yet know that he is physically separate from everything else around him that catches me. The fact that, as yet, there is no me and not-me. It all just *is*. And I feel a sudden pang of deep emotion, which is a mixture of joy for the sense of connection with all that is which he still retains, and a sense of the loss of this he is going to experience as he immerses himself more completely in the life experiences which lay ahead of him. I know he has chosen this, and I know that he is going to be fine. But just momentarily I grieve for the loss, and almost in the same moment I recognize that it is my own grief at this loss that I am feeling, and my own profound recognition of the oneness that he and I, seemingly total strangers randomly finding ourselves in the same place and at the same time, share. This so true of babies, isn't it? The way they can make us catch ourselves and fill up with emotion, bring tears to our eyes and joy to our hearts as nothing else can. It is part of the reason we all love them: they melt our hearts.

And those last few words hold the real secret about babies, don't they? They melt our hearts - a strange expression, makes it sounds like our hearts need to be unfrozen, as if they need to be softened again. What is that about? What is it that babies do to us? *For* us? I reckon that in the eyes of a baby we see a reminder of who we know ourselves to actually be. We see our own eternal beauty and radiance and zest and eagerness and loveliness reflected there. We see our actual face. We see who we were when we first came, just like this baby. We see who we really are, without all the clutter and complication of this strange reality. Without all the effort. We see beyond, and we remember. Our heart opens wide once more, and we feel the stirring of all we really are but have learned to put away.

When we look into the eyes of this newly arrived little being, we see who we really are. We see the beauty of Source in this little newly arrived being, wide open and free, ready to love and eager for adventures, fearless and curious and all joined up, not yet defended or guarded, living from the heart because the head hasn't got in the way yet. We realize, in a fluttering, fleeting moment of recognition which we can hardly express, that this little being all of us. It is pure consciousness, pure awareness, pure Love. Pure Source energy already expanding, connecting, and living fully in the moment. Moment by moment. And loving, putting no barriers in the way of love.

Love is our original energy. It is our natural state. It is what connects us, and what we are. When we remember this, just like the baby we once were, we remember that we already are completely loveable and loved, because love can be nothing else, and that we already do know, if only we will allow it, how to unconditionally love. We never really fully forget.

I wish you joyous remembering!

Traveler

Look up,
my weary friend,
bent double
with the weight
of so many
griefs,
so much
lonely disillusion,
and perceived
broken promises.
You shuffle,
eyes to the ground,
blank and unseeing
and, rootless,
you go wherever
the wind blows you.
But, my friend,
if you would only
look up.
If only you
would reach.
My hand
waits...
I cannot
insist,
only invite,
offer...ask,

in Oneness.
In recognition
of who we are.
And of the road
we both travel.
Oh my friend,
if only you would
look up,
and see.

Pain

Pain is a bit of a mixed bag, isn't it? In the long run, it can make us wiser, stronger. It can expand our ability to love unconditionally, to feel empathy and compassion, to forgive. Equally, it can leave us feeing bitter and cynical, fearful, envious, powerless. Consequently, we humans have developed a deeply ambivalent view of pain, in all its forms. We have also developed some incredibly resourceful and clever strategies for avoiding pain. Or, more accurately, for protecting ourselves from the more unpleasant effects of pain. And that really means, for avoiding the truths that life would teach us if we would allow it. We cannot have one without the other. What a difficult truth that can be.

I am not saying that tongue in cheek. I mean it when I say we are resourceful in our avoidance of pain. There are times when we need to be. We do not always feel strong enough or brave enough, or even just plain ready, to face that kind of reality. And that is okay. However, until we do face our pain, we cannot get beyond it. We cannot leave it behind. We might hear lots of very convincing arguments for not facing it, for convincing ourselves it does not exist, or for looking determinedly at the positives in everything and ignoring the negatives. But that is to miss the point. Because the point of pain is that it *is* a positive. It is the greatest learning experience we can ever have. In fact, it is the way we learn, grow, and expand. It is by working through it, integrating its effects and gifts of wisdom and understanding, and then going beyond it, that we are transformed.

Now, by pain, I do not just mean the obvious pains like grief and loss. I mean the more hidden pains, like regret, or shame. Or envy or guilt.

In many ways, the hidden nature of these makes them worse. They are so debilitating partly *because* we cannot share them easily. One of the things that saddens, and even sometimes outrages me, as a therapist, is the conspiracy of silence against being allowed to acknowledge, admit to, voice and share our pain. We all know that everyone experiences pain, and yet we must all somehow pretend it does not exist and put on a happy, smiley front to hide the truth.

I have lost count of the times a client will find the relief of tears after I have gently pointed out that they are telling me awful things, but smiling while they are telling me them, like those things are nothing because they are supposed to be nothing.

So I am going to tell you a secret about pain. It is this:

The way to find relief from pain is not to run away from it, nor to defend yourself against it. Although it is sometimes embarrassing, and bewildering, healing happens when we stop hiding from ourselves and, instead, dare to go closer. When you pull back the curtain and have a frank and honest look at what is behind there, you discover that you can look it in the face, that it will not break you, and that you can have relief. I promise you, what you will find behind there will not be even remotely as big or as bad or as ugly, as you convinced yourself that it would be while you were trying hard not to look. You might find it helpful to have someone with you when you look, or you might prefer to look on your own.

A couple of days ago, a young man came to see me. The mildest, gentlest man you could meet. He thought that what he was coming for was really silly. That it was such a little thing to cause him such problems. He apologized several times for even being there. After some encouragement and reassurance, he told me that he had a problem with shame, that he always felt like a bad person, as if he was undeserving. We talked a bit here and there, and then we got to the crux of it. I would like to share with you what he told me.

When he was little, somewhere between five and seven, his father used to put him and his sister in the bath together, and give them what he called 'toughness lessons.' When he said the words, this young man was overcome with shame, and there were tears in his eyes as I asked him to tell me about fierceness lessons. I already had a sense of the territory we were in. It seems that 'toughness lessons' involved his father making this young man, then an innocent boy, and his sister hit each other in the bath, harder and harder until they made each other cry or drew blood. And the father would have his camera with him and would take photos as they did so. He cried as he told me he had not wanted to do it. This young man, sitting in my therapy room, had carried the shame of this for over twenty years. Like it had been his fault, something unspeakable that he had done. It was only because he had at last dared to go near it, speak it, that we were able to make a different sense of it, and lift the burden of responsibility for something that clearly had not been his fault.

Shame is *always* a response to a memory of a significant other reacting to us in a way that leaves us feeling exposed or judged or humiliated. Always. And, as with all pain, once we go into it rather than away from it, then and only then can we change our perception and perspective and set ourselves free.

And here is the best thing of all about doing that: once we ourselves have dared to go towards our pain, and have discovered that it is okay, we become beacons of light and love for others who, as yet, dare not do the same. We become givers of permission and courage, givers of unconditional acceptance and freedom from judgment. Enablers and empowerers of self-love and self-respect in all with whom we come into contact. We become the loving source we always were, made manifest for all to see.

Can you see how that makes it so worthwhile? What a glorious truth to share, what a delicious liberation to offer. What a gift of love!

The voice

· ·

In stillness,
my heart's truth
speaks to me
in a voice
I can hear.
In stillness,
I am in
intimate
connection
with all that is.
And in stillness
I unleash
infinite love and healing
joy and beauty
into the world.
And in stillness,
a tender whisper:
Be still,
and know
I am that I am.
And in that moment
I hear the universe
speak my name.

Soul groups

Families can be complicated, can't they?

They can be wonderful places of refuge and strength and comfort, of support and encouragement. Places where we are known and understood and can just be ourselves without having to make too much effort. They can be energizing and uplifting places of fun and laughter and love. A wonderfully soothing, safe place of belonging. They can also be places of hurt and pain, rivalry and judgment, control and manipulation. They can be places of emotional, psychological, physical and sexual abuse or neglect or abandonment, of violence and cruelty, of endless mind games that sap our spirit and compromise our potential for happiness.

There is so much idealizing and sentimentalizing that goes on around families. For most people, the experience of being part of a family a mixed. There are family members with whom we form exceptionally strong, nurturing, and healthy bonds, and there are others we would wish rarely if ever to meet. We can carry a lot of guilt about this. It is almost taboo for someone to say they do not want to have anything to do with their father, or cannot stand to be around their mother. Or that they are tired of fighting with their brother and just need to keep their distance. It gets worse still if it is a son or daughter that someone cannot bear to be around. We hold a kind of double standard: it is okay to walk away from negative people, don't think twice before protecting yourself from anyone who brings you down or makes you unhappy; however, if it is anyone in your family, or even your entire family dynamic, that you know is harming you and causing you pain, preventing you from being the person you could be, the rules dramatically change.

However, it suddenly becomes cruel, ungrateful, inhuman, to walk away from a parent, from a sibling, from your family. You should stay at all costs, not mind the damage or hurt, remain loyal and kind, no matter what. Put yourself through Hell, even, sometimes, rather than make the choice to walk away.

So let's have a look at all this from a spiritual perspective for a moment. Let's consider the big picture, where families are concerned, and throw some much-needed light on the issues of choice and permission.

I reckon families are actually *meant* to be all those various things listed above. I reckon there are no accidents, that nothing is random, that we come into this world having fully decided, negotiated, and agreed how we want it to go. We have free will, of-course we do, and so we can change our minds whenever we want and do any of it differently, but essentially, we have chosen the families we will be born into, prior to incarnating, and the family members involved, as their higher selves, have equally volunteered to incarnate along with us.

These generous souls have also agreed to live out their lives playing the particular roles we have asked them to play out for us. Similarly, we also have agreed to play out a particular role for them. And together, we will build the experiences that we have come intending to experience in this lifetime. This is true of everyone with whom we have contact, interaction or relationships, in any particular lifetime, but just for now let us think purely about families. In addition, let us think of families in terms of soul groups. We are so familiar with pictures of happy groups laughing and having fun together, with captions on them saying how wonderful it is when we recognize or meet up with members of our soul family. And we ourselves celebrate how wonderful it is when we recognize each other and remember the bond we have forged through many lifetimes. What we do not tend to see - because we like to stay determinedly away from such realities - but which would be just as true, and every bit as appropriate, are pictures of families falling out and in difficulty. Also with captions on them making reference to soul families. We perpetuate the idea that soul family always gets along, and is always happy and supportive and having fun.

But soul family is way more wonderful than that. Way more amazing. It's one thing to agree to meet up again and have fun and be loved; it's quite another to agree to meet up again and play the role of the bad guy, to agree to help you learn a lesson or go through an experience which is knowingly going to be immensely painful. And which, just for this lifetime - since the members of our soul family, as their higher selves, are Love, and can be no other - will bring us into painful conflict, and even estrangement.

When you look at it from this perspective, isn't this the most incredibly generous and loving act? To agree to incarnate in order to play out a difficult scenario with us, simply because we have asked it? Isn't it equally amazing, if we reverse this, that we have also agreed to do the same - to play out a role, or be the instigator of a difficult experience, for a parent, or our parents or our family, in order that expansion and growth can happen? Because expansion happens through contrast, through experiencing and surviving challenging and conflicted situations. If there were only joy and fun there would be no expansion.

So, how about we let ourselves, and our parents, or siblings, or families, off the hook. And partners and children too. And how about we just embrace the experience, without blame and without guilt, for what it is: a cooperative co-creation for the expansion of all concerned. Can you feel the freedom of that? We cannot get it wrong, because everything is a lesson; everything is expansion, Source experiencing every aspect of what it is to be human. All of it, not just the 'good' bits. Whatever roles we are playing out, that is all they are, merely roles. We can know that we will all meet up again when it is all done, and have a good old laugh and reflect on it all, from the viewpoint not of this limited time/place reality, but of the greater wisdom and loving compassion which we actually are.

Once we really take this on board, in time there can eventually be an understanding of the lengths to which someone has been willing to go on our behalf. And an acknowledgement of the part we ourselves have played in another's expansion, knowing that it was planned and agreed. Not the detail. But certainly the intention. In Love and Oneness.

Wow, how awesome we all are!

You are the space

. . . .

You are the space
that holds
all of humanity.
You allow
the entire river
of human consciousness
to flow
through you.
You are nothing
and at the same time
everything.
Everything you breathe
is also
breathing you.
You are the One
and the All.
You are the space
in which everything moves,
and you are the flow
within which everything exists.
You are the observer
and the observed,
the experience
and the One experiencing.
You are the nothing
that holds everything.

For lightworkers everywhere

For all those of us who struggle with boundaries, I hope this distinction may prove helpful:

The difference between *empathy* and *identifying*....is the difference between observing someone drowning with compassion and keeping the other company from the solid ground on the shore....and jumping in shouting, 'Let's drown together.'

One of the things that young therapists in training find it hardest to learn is the difference between empathy and identification. For several years I was responsible for training young therapists on a university M.A, and so I know what a struggle everyone found it to pull out of getting so wrapped up in the other's material sufficiently in order to actually be useful rather than adding to the drama. I mention this because I think that it is a challenge many of us face. I am speaking of those of us, just like the students I am describing, who cannot help becoming identified with the experience of the person we are speaking with. It can be a bit of a nightmare. I have known people tell me they dread going out because they know they will come back dripping with other people's projections, or split off feelings and experiences.

Some of us go around telling the world we are an empath, and we can more or less make a virtue of the fact that we feel what others feel, and can see inside their heads. We can be conned into thinking that this is how it is supposed to be. However, we then go on to describe what we see as the inevitable downside of what some of us call a gift, and others a curse. We say that we suffer horribly in crowds or when we are around other people, never know peace, cannot sort out what are our own feelings and what are the feelings of other people. Suddenly, it is not so great. So I thought that maybe it might be helpful to say something about the very important distinction between empathizing and identifying. One is healthy; the other is unhelpful and leads to our becoming ill. It is helpful in general, but particularly vital knowledge for those of us who would call ourselves lightworkers. We tend to be called empaths.

So, first, here's the bad news. It is where we have to start. It is perhaps going to be a shock to some, but we need to begin at the beginning: empaths are not empathizing, they are actually identifying. I repeat, empaths are not empathizing, they are identifying. They have lost their observer self (the one who stays on the shore reassuring the other) and instead have plunged into the water and are flailing around waving their arms in the air shouting, 'Help, we're both drowning!'

Those of us who grew up learning to be empaths (identifiers) usually grew up with either an over-anxious parent, who couldn't manage their own feelings very well. We consequently became responsible for taking them into us instead - or a pretty shut down parent, who could give us little or no help in managing our own feelings, because they simply did not do feelings. In the first case - that of an over-anxious parent - we were required to become what is called, in my theoretical background, a 'container' for that parent, because that parent could not act as a container for themselves. We are not talking blame here, just cause and effect. If you cannot contain your own feelings, you look for someone else to contain them for you. In this case, your child. You. Trouble is, a child does not have the resources to be a container for someone else's feelings, because a child only learns how to contain their own feelings when a parent capable of managing *their* own feelings shows them how. You see how complicated this is getting?

So then, back to the second scenario - a parent who is emotionally shut down. For different reasons, this parent is also unable to show a child how to contain their feelings. Instead of knowing how to do this themselves, they have discovered what seems like a safe alternative, which is to push them all away out of sight and shut down. This is called splitting. Psychically, we split off our unwanted and unacknowledged feelings unconsciously, and put them into someone else. Typically, these two parents can often show up together, so that we have one parent who is emotionally overflowing and another who is emotionally shut down. Remember, we are not allocating any blame here - these parents are the way they are because of the parenting they themselves received, which clearly also gave little help with how to manage feelings.

So back to the child. Without help to either contain or process feelings - which are pretty big and frightening things to a child - this child is now exposed to feelings and images in the raw; wild feelings, if you like, with no help to know how to tame them. As the child develops, feelings can remain frightening, a threat rather than a friend, an attacker rather than an ally. Moreover, feelings and images continue to hold quite nightmarish proportions, and we have a fearful relationship with them, particularly those we receive from other people. This child then grows to adulthood with few emotional or psychic boundaries - remember, they were, and most likely still are, used as an emotional and psychic container for a parent, and so healthy boundaries, the line between self and other, were given no opportunity to form. Instead, they exist in a state of readiness to absorb and merge, rather like a psychic or emotional sponge. This is not 'oneness', before anyone suggests that. This is most certainly not healthy. For anyone.

Now, you might say, but is that not the role of an empath? Aren't we here to rescue the human race from itself by reading other people's feelings and projections? Is that not part of our gift to the world? And I would say, but how does it help someone to drown with them? It makes them responsible for trying to save not only themselves from drowning, but you, as well. What the world needs, and I am talking spiritually here now, as well as emotionally and psychically, is not more empaths, but more transmuters. I am talking lightworker talk.

We know, many of us, that everything is light, and that we are beings of light. We know that the only difference between one expression or manifestation of light and another is the frequency at which it vibrates. We also know that light must flow freely and that when that flow is interrupted or held up, blockages and stagnant, stuck energy results. We know that where such blockages or stagnant energy occurs, either the flow must be restored, or the energy transmuted. That is, transformed vibrationally into a more healthy frequency. A better feeling, in our context.

Now, back to the child who became the adult, who is an empath. Since that child is absorbing, pretty constantly, raw, unprocessed, stuck energy – because there was no one else available who could deal with it; and since they themselves have little capacity to do more than receive it, having been given no help to know how to do more - their own energy systems are going to be pretty blocked, and they are going to find that they are emotionally and psychically all over the place, busy carrying the stuff that no-one else wants. And probably getting ill pretty frequently too. It doesn't sound too great when you look at it like that, does it?

So, the biggy: what do you do instead? Here are my own thoughts on that. They are just my thoughts, and I make no claim that they are anything more than thoughts. Still, I hope they maybe have some use. Supposing you were to do the following: You begin to process and transmute the energy you receive, rather than merely absorbing it. You become what you were meant to be. A lightworker who knows their purpose. A lightworker who transmutes light vibrationally. A lightworker who takes light that is vibrating at a low frequency and transmutes it into energy vibrating at the highest frequency possible: that of love. We might not put it in those terms always, but that *is* what a lightworker does. A lightworker is an empath with muscle.

In practice, that means we would cease going around absorbing everyone's unwanted emotion, and instead we would start going round learning to tell what is ours and what is not, and releasing what is not, wIth enormous love and understanding and compassion - with *true empathy* - to the Universe. We would get smart, we would get knowing, we would become *aware*. We would stop feeling fearful and start being loving instead. Radiating outwards such love and compassion that any low vibrational energy with which we come into contact cannot fail to be transmuted into that same frequency of love.

Can you see what that could do? Can you catch the excitement of that? Can you see it? Can you see how a planet where loving souls were consciously transmuting energy they received, that others couldn't deal with, but which they did know how to deal with, could become transformed? We would no longer do it by accident, a bit hit and miss. We would do it consciously, in awareness, with purpose. And through that, we would bring enormous power to this planet, and we would keep the flow going. This is the true gift of an empath, who has been transformed into a lightworker.

We've served our apprenticeships. Now let's show the world what we're made of!

Shame

. . . .

Shame is
Source
experiencing
the vulnerability
of being
human.
A wonderful
meeting place
of the known
and the not yet known,
of remembering
in a moment
of shock
what we had forgotten.
Nothing more.
All is as it should be.
Let go.

The creation of reality

Very many of us like to ask for protection, to be kept safe by someone or something external, and more powerful than we are... We pray and we use ritual, or a talisman, maybe. A lucky charm. It does not really matter what it is. What we are really wanting is to feel the comfort of knowing that something, or someone, 'out there' is watching over us and will not let anything 'bad' happen to us. We like to feel protected. We want to feel safe. It feels comforting to give the responsibility for that to someone else 'out there.'

However, when we do that, aren't we perhaps missing the point? We are buying into the belief that we are 'here' and the energy we like to call "Source" or 'Spirit' is 'there.' We are talking as if we are different energies, different beings. We are not remembering, not allowing the realization that we *are* this energy, all of us: that this energy breathes in time with us, sees through our eyes, and is the beating of our heart. That there is a place inside us where we have always known, and are known. That there is no distinction, no separation, that we are *all one*.

Initially, you might panic and think, 'That means I'm on my own in all this, it's down to me, and me alone!' However, that would be the ego getting scared. The bit of you which takes on the role you decide to adopt during this incarnation, and plays that role exceptionally well for you. The ego, as planned and agreed, is convinced of its separateness, its separation, because the ego has amnesia. It is the device that makes experiencing life in this temporary time/space reality possible. If there were no amnesia, there could be no expansion. You cannot engage fully in a reality you know is just a game; you must completely believe it.

But the amnesia does not have to last, and it does not have to mean we feel alone. It certainly does not mean that we are alone. And our remembering is every bit as important a part of expansion as is our forgetting. There is nothing that does not contribute to, and facilitate, expansion. We are Source energy, and therefore Source itself. All of us, and all that is. Because there is nothing that is not Source. Source is everywhere and everything. And the nature of Source is Love Expanding. Therefore, we are never alone, we are intimately and intrinsically connected and in communication at all times with All That Is. Why would Source feel the need to protect itself?

Do you see how safe you are? Do you see how every breath you take is being taken with you? That it is such a very tender shared breath, in love and in oneness? Source breathing through you? Source seeing through your eyes? Do you begin to see what you are, and how powerful you are Everything that feels like it is happening to you is actually happening inside the Awareness of Source? You are witnessing this experiencing. You are creating the experience, not the victim of it.

You have everything you need, and you *are* everything you need. All you need do is remember. You will know you are remembering because it will feel wholly right. Your body will feel it and your inner being will tell you. You are infinitely powerful, because Source - which you are - is infinitely powerful. You are infinite compassion, because Source - which you are - is infinite compassion. You are infinite wisdom, because Source - which you are - is infinite wisdom. You are unconditional Love, because Source - which you are - is unconditional Love.

You are Source having a human experience as Love Expanding. And the wonderful thing is, now you *know it*! Allow yourself to sink into the enormity of that, and have a truly great day!

See

Each moment
is completely fresh,
new made,
trembling
in anticipation
of being seen.

Did you see?

In defense of defenses

I want to speak up on behalf of some much-maligned friends of ours, which we have labelled 'Defenses.' I would like to champion them a bit.

We like to knock defenses. We like to say, confidently, that defenses are a 'bad thing' and a trick of the egoic mind. We give them quite a bashing, as if they are somehow the primary block to our getting in 'proper' touch with 'reality.' And yes, of course that is true - the bit about them being a trick. They trick us into perceiving the world a certain way. They take away some or other intolerably painful aspect of our apparent reality, and replace it with a more comforting perception of our apparent reality. And I say 'apparent reality' on purpose, since we are not at any point 'in touch' with any absolute 'reality', ever, since such a thing simply doesn't exist...does it?

So, while I wholeheartedly agree that defenses change our perception of reality, and that this *can* be unhelpful, I want to reconsider the bit about them always being the 'bad guys' which must be eliminated at all costs in the interests of our becoming 'fully real.' Whatever *that* means. The bit about them coming from the egoic mind. I want to let us off the hook a bit, give us permission to go a little easier on ourselves. And I want to try to help us all feel some healthy appreciation for our defenses, without which none of us would have survived intact in this pretty challenging time/place reality. I do not want to change or soften that statement. I will even say it again. Without our defenses, none of us would have survived in this pretty challenging time/place reality.

Let me give you an example of what I mean; let me tell you about a little girl we can call Jane. I'm going to tell it just like it is, and so I'm going to use words which are simply intended to give an accurate picture, but which might initially seem judgmental. It is all simply as it is, and as it was. So bear with me. Let me tell you some of what happened to her when she was newly here...

Jane's mother was a quite tortured woman, who struggled with both major depression, and interludes of psychosis, where she lost touch with 'reality. Her own childhood had been difficult for her, with a controlling and intrusive mother and a cold and volatile father. She therefore had little or no knowledge of being held, soothed, or unconditionally loved. Moreover, she carried inside her such a gaping emptiness that she often could not bear, to the point where she would leave reality for a while and become psychotic. Jane's father had been through World War 1, and had come back a changed and haunted man. He had shut down emotionally in order to not remember.

When Jane was fifteen months old, her mother had a major psychotic breakdown, after deteriorating steadily for many months. Having a baby was overwhelming for her; she could not meet her own needs let alone those of a baby. And Jane's father, for whom this was so reminiscent of the madness which had been war, shut down even more and withdrew, leaving what small extended family there was on Jane's mother's side, to pick up the pieces. You will already be noticing defenses galore going on here, and you will have all sorts of feelings and perceptions going on about what is happening here, maybe. However, let us just see this through.

So now, here is Jane.

Without warning, and clearly without any digestible explanation being able to be given, Jane's mother suddenly, and completely, disappears from her life, after having been admitted to hospital. She is there for nearly a year. Jane's father also collapses and disappears. Jane has been told by other family members that she was inconsolable for several weeks, sobbing every night, alone in her cot, and often for periods through the day, calling for her mummy. An elderly aunt was brought in to look after her, who believed in leaving children to cry and teaching them not to be demanding or make a fuss. And so, when Jane cried, she was not cuddled or consoled. Instead, she was left to 'soothe herself.'

Then, one day, Jane simply stopped. She stopped crying, and she stopped calling for her mummy. She became silent. She stopped reacting. She stopped feeling. She stopped seeing because she had stopped looking. Her eyes glazed over and became blank. And the pain went away. I want to tell you what Jane did which made the pain go away: Jane changed her perception of reality.

A little psyche, less than two years on this earth, changed her perception of reality. She decided to perceive reality in the following way:

+ She does not need her mummy; she is self-sufficient
+ Loving and needing is dangerous because it makes people go away
+ She must have done something really bad to make her mummy go away and her daddy stop loving her
+ It therefore is not her mummy or daddy who is to blame here, but her
+ Crying and reaching out, calling out, asking for help brings no response or help, and so you have to manage on your own in this hostile world
+ From now on, she will not allow anyone or anything to matter, and she will keep herself from harm and any further pain

Jane thus develops what we therapists recognize as a schizoid defense. And she also develops the internal conflict that she will spend a lifetime working out: she will long for intimate relationship while being terrified of it at the same time. And now, here is Jane, the grown up woman she was destined to become:

She comes to see me because she is frustrated, at the end of her tether. Every single time that something that could be a really exciting opportunity comes along, she sabotages it. She either takes no action at all, so that by default, it passes her by, or she makes some excuse and runs hard and fast in the opposite direction. Commitment terrifies her. If friends move job or to a different part of the country, she quietly cuts them off. She does the same with any romantic relationship. The first time they let her down, they are out. There are no grey areas, ever. It is all very black and white. She knows she is doing it, she wishes she did not do it, but she cannot manage it any other way. Jane is really good fun, charming, and people love the way she can be entertaining and make them laugh.

However, Jane knows that she is just putting on a very convincing act, putting on a show. She does not allow anyone to get too close. Ever.

'But *why* can't I do it differently?' Jane throws up her hands in frustration and despair. 'I want to scream at myself, "Here you go again! After all these years, you are still doing it! When are you going to bloody well start living your life? Really living it!" 'Her voice is full of self-loathing and contempt. Jane despises herself. Yet when she looks at me, behind the steely anger, her eyes are brimming with tears.

Jane is ready. She wants this to stop. She wants relief. She has taken the all-important first step. She has reached out to another human being. And so the journey of therapy begins. It doesn't have to be therapy. There are an infinite number of ways. But Jane has chosen therapy, and the relationship, the experience of relationship, will bring her the ability to heal. Crucially, it will help her to remember, to make sense of what's going on, let it go, and forgive herself. Because *that* is the crucial bit. We must understand and become aware, we must see what we are doing and why - because only then do we have true expansion - with compassion and kindness, and then we must forgive ourselves.

So back to defenses, and why they are not the bad guys. Why they are, in fact, our best and most intimate allies. Without the defenses which her source allowed and encouraged her to put in place as a tiny little girl, Jane could not and would not have survived. She would have gone mad or she would have lost the will to live. I mean that literally, I am not exaggerating or being dramatic. Jane's defenses saved her sanity and her life. They also reveal the way that this little newly arrived being, fresh from Source and so, so powerful a creator, manages her reality in order that she can bring herself safely through, intact, to the point at which she is ready to consciously and knowingly appreciate her own expansion.

And part of that process involves looking at her story, and learning to marvel at it rather than beating herself up. To look at the amazing survivor she is, how cleverly and intricately she has woven and developed the story she had decided to play out in this lifetime. To appreciate the skill and the courage it has taken. To stand in awe of her creation. And, from that place of knowing, to forgive herself. We are all on this same path. We came in search of contrast and expansion. However, we also came with a safety net. Because we wanted it to be bearable. At its worse, we needed to know it would be bearable. And that is because we come from Love, and Love does not require suffering, and Love demands that there should always be help and relief. And so Love provides us with defenses. And when we are ready, we let them go. In Love and with enormous appreciation for their wonderful gift of protection.

I don't believe that defenses are a function of the ego; I believe they are a gift of the divine. And when we look at them in that way, we can celebrate our amazing creative power, the far reach of our incredible imagination, our resilience and determination and courage out here on the leading edge. And we can forgive ourselves for temporarily forgetting that this is what we were doing all the time!

Storm

· ·

I cried out in the
middle of the storm:
I cannot do this,
it is too much,
do not ask it.
And the voice whispered:
This too shall pass.
Let it be.
All is as it should be.
All is well.

I cried out as the rain
lashed and drenched
and chilled me
to the bone:
I am not strong enough,
I cannot withstand it,
this will wash me away,
I will drown in it.
And the voice whispered:
You are strong,
you are powerful,
stand firm and it will
wash over you.
This too shall pass.

Let go, let be.
All is as it should be.
All is well.

I gasped as the wind
took my breath away,
tearing and swirling and raging,
almost knocking me over.
Struggling to stay
on my feet,
I cried out in fear:
I need this to stop
I cannot hold on
I must let go soon.
And the voice whispered,
Your roots are deeper
than you think,
and you are far wiser
than you think.
Bend and turn and let go.
This too shall pass.
Let this flow and move through you.
All is exactly as it needs to be.
All is well.

I cried more tears
than I knew I had inside me,
and sobbed more protests
than I knew were in me.
I became the storm,
I became the rain,
raged with the wind itself.
I gave myself up,

I let go and became one
with each moment,
as the storm whipped
into a frenzy.
I held on and held on,
as I shook and bent and turned
and broke and yielded.
And let go...
And let go...

And finally,
finally, finally...
at long last
the storm began to ease,
the sky became kinder,
the rain fell more gently.
The wind became a breeze,
warm and gentle
tender and soothing
and I remembered
all the voice had whispered.
And I knew
that I was not only the storm,
and the rain and the wind,
but the voice also.
I knew that the voice
was mine,
and yet not mine alone
but our voices,
countless voices.
All of us.
One voice.

I knew that where I had been
we all had been,
where I was, we all were.
And that where I now stood
we were all now standing.
I remembered this voice
down the ages, beyond and beneath and in all.
And I let go.
And let be.
And let be.

Wanting

· ·

One of the most painful and bewildering experiences I come up against in the therapy room is wanting. We put a lot of energy into wanting things, don't we? It takes up a great deal of our thinking and feeling, and it causes us a great deal of suffering.

We want to be successful; we want the perfect job, the perfect relationship. Money, lots of money, more money. Happiness. More happiness. More. More. We are often really confused and muddled about it. What we want keeps changing. It is never quite right, never quite enough. It never satisfies because it is never quite perfect. So we keep trying, keep going, hoping that sooner or later we will find what it is we need. It becomes a mission, for happiness, but grows ever more confusing. We want something, and then we want the opposite. Or we want something but feel we shouldn't want it really. Or we were fine until someone happened to tell us about something they wanted, and now we want it too.

Moreover, wanting causes us a fair amount of suffering and confusion. If we don't have what we want, we suffer from the sense of lack of it and the consequent wanting as we long for what we don't have. If we get what we want, we suffer because, now we have what we were wanting, we find it only makes us want more. Or we find that it is not what we thought it would be when we were wanting it. We are on an endless round of wanting, rejecting, being disappointed, wishing we didn't want, wanting more, wanting something different, wanting something better.

The wanting never stops. If anything, it increases, taking up an increasing amount of our time. We focus on wanting, more and more. And then to top it all, we are told we can have anything we want as long as we no longer allow ourselves to want it. As long as we make it not matter to us anymore. Of-course, psychologically, this simply makes us either want it even more, or turn our attention to wanting something else instead so that we do not think about the thing we want so badly that we must under no circumstances think about it. It does not stop the wanting. If anything, it intensifies it.

The fundamental problem is this kind of wanting causes us such problems because wanting comes from the ego. That old friend we keep talking about that so beautifully and effectively aids our expansion. The ego is always dissatisfied because it is fear-based. The nature of the fear-based ego is to perceive lack. It is never at peace, never content. When we are seeing our world through the ego's eyes, which we initially come here to do, we will always be convinced that more will make us happy. This thing. Or the next thing. Then the next.

Spiritual teachings and self-help books on law of attraction can also encourage this position, if we are not consciously aware of the ego trap, and being careful not to fall into it. We are encouraged to focus our attention on the fact that we can have *anything* we want. To believe that getting what we want will make us happy. That happiness will be ours once we have the things we are encouraged to want. Thing is, happiness never was about getting things, never will be. That is one of the biggest cons out - and there are quite a few!

Eventually, as we become more aware, more awake, we start to see what a cleverly concocted myth this was. We begin to see through eyes that are more spiritual rather than eyes fixed firmly on getting what we want. We start to expand in a new way. Our eyes start to clear. We start to awaken to love for self and other, rather than trying to fill the space with things that do not satisfy. We start to focus on oneness rather than me-ness, compassion rather than selfishness. We realize we do not need to want, because Source always provides. And that we are source energy, always connected to abundance and wellbeing. We come to appreciate that we do not need to strive so hard because, once we stop striving, we discover that life flows abundantly to us, and there is plenty to go round.

However, there is another kind of wanting beyond this wanting. We get beyond the belief that success and possessions will make us happy, but then we start wanting our life and circumstances to be different. We feel regret and longing, we play the 'if only this had happened' or the 'if only this would happen' game. And in doing so, we reach a further layer of discontent, and cause ourselves even more unhappiness. We are still operating, whenever we find ourselves wanting in this way, from a place of fear. Why is wanting fear-based? Simply because to want is to not trust that everything will happen exactly as we need it to. Because inside wanting there is still a focus on lack, and a not being quite sure whether or not the universe is listening and is going to heed our request. Trust, in contrast, being love-based, is able to appreciate the moment, enjoy what is, and revel in the delicious anticipation of blessings on their way, because trust knows they will be coming.

And the amazing fact is that, once we allow ourselves to fall in to this place of trust and contentment, of grace and ease, then that is when the real miracles start to happen.

Because, you know what, despite all our wanting, all our striving, we don't have the capacity to even begin to imagine all that can come to us once we get out of our own way. Once we realize we don't have to want, because everything we have agreed prior to incarnating is already in place for us, and we do not have to do anything, we can just allow the wonderful flow of that, rest in the certainty of that, and leave room for the really satisfying things. Just enjoy what is. Here and now. Like connection, relationship, generosity and kindness, understanding and compassion, and gratitude and appreciation. Like joy, and peace, and excitement, beauty and wonder.

Like love. Most of all, like love.

Now before any of this is misinterpreted, no one is saying that it is wrong to want good things for yourself, for those you love, for the world. Rather, it is that good things come far more readily and abundantly - and quickly - when we are not focused on them from the ego. The power, and the magical pull of love is way more powerful than anything fear and lack can ever produce. And there lies spiritual freedom and personal liberation, and wholeness.

That has to be a good thing... don't you agree?

Inner being

Your inner being
is forever
talking to you.
It never shouts.
That is not its way.
It is the small voice
in the midst of stillness
and the whisper in the wind.
It is in the shapes of clouds
and the signs of nature.
It is in the sensations
in your body
and the stories
unfolding in your dreams.
Listen, and it will tell you
all you need to know.

The importance of feeling

A high proportion of those who are sufficiently troubled to seek the help of another, and who find their way to my therapy room, have little or no sense of what they are feeling. When we find ourselves overwhelmed in life, or by life, we can feel either numb or shut down, or so full of emotion that all we can feel is a heightened sensation of anxiety or panic. This is always frightening, bewildering, and leaves anyone in either of these places feeling lost, alone, ungrounded, and out of control.

In reality, what is happening is that we have lost touch with what we are actually feeling, and we are experiencing the physical effects on the body of such loss of connection. Being out of touch with our feelings means being out of touch with who we are, out of touch with our source. So let us look at what that actually means, and what the consequences are.

The only way we ever know how we are doing - some of us would talk about our vibration, some of us would refer to our emotional health, others to our spiritual well-being - the language does not matter as much as the meaning - is by how we *feel*. Right now in this moment. And now. And again, now. Our feelings are in constant flux, constant flow. And our nature is to be experiencers, witnessers, noticers. When we do not know how we feel, we do not know who we are, where we have come from, or where we are going. We are suspended in a semi-conscious reality where there is only thinking, or the attempt to think, of purely reacting rather than observing, but no sense of the emotional life which is so crucial to our wellbeing and awareness, and which is the vital link that connects us to our source.

In western society, we tend to be taught either that emotions are untrustworthy - we should only trust logic - or dangerous - they get us into trouble, make us get carried away, hurt people, leave us vulnerable. We like to steer clear of anything that might open us up to feeling, and try instead to solve our emotional problems by building up our ability to train our thought patterns to prevent us from feeling what we feel. We even create confusion about feelings that are specific to each gender: girls must not get angry; boys must not get upset; girls must be kind and sympathetic, boys must be strong. As a result, we become rather left-brained and one-sided. We work really hard to remain totally rational, and we to try to resist, and even come to despise, anything 'irrational' which comes into our head. Note: head. Not heart. This is all about the head.

We even get ourselves in a muddle by mixing up thoughts and feelings. We think they are the same, and we use the words as though they are interchangeable. You hear it all the time. 'I feel like I have made an awful mistake.' Actually, this is really: 'I *think* I have made an awful mistake.' What you are probably *feeling* is worried, frightened. We do not know the difference any more, but a thought is an activity that takes place in the head, and then filters down into the body; a feeling is an activity that takes place in the heart and then filters out into the body and is eventually registered in the head.

Because of the taboo on feelings, and the emphasis on logic and the rational, we are taught to cut off our inner guidance, our direct link to our source. Therefore, instead of knowing what we *feel* we want, or what we do not want, we try to *think* what we *should* want or what we *ought* to want. This makes it incredibly hard for us to work out how we are, who we are, why we are. And it makes it hard for us to be tuned in or switched on to what our source is telling us. Listening to our inner voice, or intuition, requires that we are aware of what we are feeling, emotionally and physically.

There are only two basic emotions: love and fear. Everything else is either a defense against feeling one or other of these, or a variation on one or other of these. Love comes from connecting with Source energy; fear comes from cutting ourselves off from Source energy. It really is that simple. When we try to stick solely with logic, we are ceasing to listen to our source. We switch off our intuition. We get into a strange tangle where we believe that someone or something 'out there' is making us respond, behave, or react in a certain way. We say things like, 'She makes me feel angry,' or 'He makes me feel anxious.' This is upside down, wrong way round 'in the head' talk.

If we were in touch fully with our source, we would be saying, 'I feel angry when I am with her and she does/says that,' or 'I feel anxious around him.' We would be owning what we feel because we would be in touch with ourselves well enough to know that these feelings originate in us, and not 'out there.' When we are not used to noticing, acknowledging, and processing our feelings, we experience life as if things 'out there' are making us feel things. We do not understand that our reactions to things happen within us, and that it is our responsibility to locate and own them.

If we stay connected to how we feel, we start to actually experience that, if we listen to, and are aware of, our feelings moment to moment, we can always find our way out of a bad place, where we are disconnected from Source, and find our way back into alignment, or connection. We discover that, by remembering how good a particular emotional place feels, and recalling the emotion of that so accurately that it is live in us once again; we can actually get ourselves back there. We learn that we have power and choice, are not the victim of external circumstances, but rather the observer of the experience and our reaction to it. It is always an inside job. It always has been. We are, after all, powerful creators who, through the vibrational footprint being emitted by our emotional energy, are moment by moment creating the nature of our reality.

What freedom and relief there is in that, once we really understand it and get it. Nothing in the outside world has to change, or needs to change, in order for us to feel good. We already have all the tools we need. Our emotions are key. Ultimately, once we start to discover just how powerful this insider knowledge is, we are unstoppable. We simply have to get back in touch with who we really are - Source energy, Love and Light energy, connected through our senses and feelings. Here to experience the full range of what it is to be human.

To live in the heart and not just the head.

Supposing, just supposing, that enough of us started to do that, to make the language of feeling, and the expressing of it, central in our day to day lives, and to encourage others to do that, that we began a quiet revolution, a return to living in the heart. What a ride that could be! What a rollercoaster of a ride of an adventure!

Renewal

· ·

Leave behind
the clatter
and the clutter
and sit quietly,
soulfully,
at the feet
of the one
who birthed you
and who sustains
your every breath.
Feel her arms
enfold you
with the wisdom
of the ages,
and her gentle
vibrant energy
pulse once again
through the core
of you.
Come home,
and be renewed.

Memory feelings

· ·

It happens more times than we realize. We are busy going about our ordinary everyday life when suddenly, without being aware of it, our mind is not here at all. And because our mind is not here, neither are we. No matter what our mood was a moment ago, it can have completely switched. We are some other place, some other time, in some other feeling. Often, we are a different age, in a different place and situation. And, just like a rabbit caught in the headlights, we are mesmerized.

The mind remembers unhappy times or traumatic times far more readily than it does pleasant times. This is because, at the time of their happening, they have a far greater impact on our energetic and neural system than do happy experiences. That means that the 'place' we are often caught in takes us straight to a place of fear or dread or pain or shame and we are caught or frozen in the moment, as memory feeling replaces current feeling.

It is not always an unpleasant memory, of-course. There are those delicious moments when we are lifted out of ourselves by recalling something heart-warming or funny or delightful or joyous, and those moments leave us caught in the headlights in a very different way. Usually with a huge grin on our face that leaves everyone puzzled as to what we are thinking about. However, those other times, when we feel our confidence slip away, the words dry up in our mouth, maybe a sense of self-consciousness, or unknown dread flood us, when we feel like a child again, helpless, those debilitating moments, what is that? I use the term 'memory feelings' to make sense of these. I picture all we have known and experienced as a huge glistening web, each thread of which is a kind of experience we have had, a theme of our life, if you like. Where the threads meet or cross are moments of significant experience, the defining moments, the moments which can be triggered whenever something happens now which is similar to what it was that happened back then.

Whenever there is a flavour *now*, in the present moment, of something we experienced *back then*, the web vibrates. We feel the vibration as returning memory, and the web we are standing on shakes beneath our feet. We find ourselves temporarily wobbling, not feeling grounded, our consciousness drawn to that intersection in the web, right over there, which is shaking us up over here.

However, if we use this image, all we need to do is take the bounce and then steady the momentum of the vibration until it is still again. A bit like we might do on a trampoline. We bend our knees, we stay steady and grounded, we breathe and bring calm, and the movement stills. In the moment, 'bending our knees and steadying the momentum of the web' in practical terms means using mindful awareness to come back to *now*.

Notice where you are, who you are, your surroundings now, sounds now, textures and scents now, and remind yourself where you are. Become completely grounded in *now*, and then use the breath to get back fully the essence of all you are now, rather than being lost in the essence of who you once were. Remind yourself that you are powerful now, have choice now, and are free now, can speak now, can stay or walk away now. That no one any longer has control over you, can hurt you or frighten you; that you and you alone, give yourself permission. No one else.

And you tell yourself that these were memory feelings only. Not real now. Not relevant now. Without power now. Just a vibration of the web, nothing more.

And you smile, and think, oh that's all right then. All is well!

The Awakening

Precious traveler,
do not dwell too long
in that place
we call
The Dark Night of the Soul.
It is a brief vigil only
which you yourself
hold
in the sacred space
before the portal,
which always then opens
and shows you
the way
to the pure essence
of who you are.
You think it is a loss
of all you have held dear
and certain.
You fear you will break.
You think you are losing yourself
and your truth,
or that there is no truth,
that there is nothing,
and that all has been in vain.
But we, those who walk with you,
have always walked with you
from the beginning,

and who have always loved you
and always known you,
we hold here for you all you seek.
This is no empty quest.
You do it for all, and with all.
And we tread every step,
and share every breath, with you.
The Awakening
will be glorious.
And you will laugh once more,
And dance with us all
Amongst the stars!

On forgiveness

Over the years, one of the questions which has most troubled those who have sat in my therapy room has been, 'How do I forgive?'

When people say this, they do not usually mean, 'It was such a horrendous thing I can't possibly forgive it. Ever.' Sometimes they do, and that is a decision they must be free to make. What they generally mean is, 'I want to forgive, but I don't know how. Everywhere I look, I read and hear that I need to forgive in order to move on. And I want to do that. Badly. But I simply don't know how.' For anyone who would welcome some thoughts about the 'How to' of forgiving, these are the four stages I have come to believe we have to go through in order to feel the release and relief of forgiveness:

1. We must fully acknowledge and allow our memories and feelings of the events or situation we are wanting to forgive. If we do not do this, we do not properly know what it is we are trying to forgive, and those experiences will come back to trip us up again and again.
2. We must understand that our memories and feelings are valid. We must not try to deny, rationalize, or push away what our experience was. This is not to wallow, or be full of self-pity, not a 'poor me' exercise. We are intending to allow feelings which the child or adult we were needs to be heard and acknowledged. If we do not do this, those unacknowledged feelings fester.
3. We must understand as fully as possible, and emphatically appreciate, how it was for the other/others whom we are wanting to forgive. We must see what happened through their eyes. We

must appreciate how complex it all was. Hurt is never simple, neither are circumstances or intentions.

4. Finally, we must reach a place where we can see the lessons we learned, the growth that has happened as a result of the experience we are wanting to forgive. And having identified those, we must be appreciative of that experience/situation for the gifts it has given us.

5. If it resonates for us spiritually, we can also remind ourselves that everyone in the situation was playing a pre-agreed role for each other, and that its message, meaning, and purpose will become clear, and will be a blessing.

This is a pretty full and demanding and comprehensive process, but necessary. Sometimes we can accomplish it in moments; sometimes it can take years. However and whenever, when we forgive we free ourselves from a weighty burden, and the experience of true and lasting relief is joyous!

I Am

Whatever unfolds,
whatever opens or closes,
is found or is lost,
is discovered or forgotten,
what begins or has its ending,
is a delight or a wound,
I look on and I watch the play,
both the player and the director.
And in every moment
I know that I am both
the change and changeless.
That I am the observer and the observed
The creator and what is being created.
The breather and the breath.
Always, I remain
the stillness in the chaos.
Always I AM.

On empathy

A great deal has been written about 'sensitive souls.' We often call them 'empaths': how you know if you are one, how to recognize negative energy from others, how to clear negative energy, how to protect yourself. I thought it might be helpful to offer some additional thoughts. For those for whom they resonate, I hope you will find them helpful. They are my thoughts only; I am adding to, not taking away from, what others have already said.

One: we are all empaths; it varies only by degree. If you think about how large our energy fields actually are, around ten to twenty feet or more, you will get an idea of how frequently our energy fields touch and overlap. Think about that. We cannot escape each other's energy. In any case, we are all the same energy, and so separateness is an illusion of convenience, nothing more.

Two: Let us think about this spiritually for a few moments. We all talk about duality. We all seem to agree that fear-based thinking is unhelpful. So why do we suddenly jump on the fear-based wagon when it comes to coming into contact with energy which, in any particular given moment, does not belong to us? How come we start smudging ourselves from head to toe, and every room in the house, like we love-based creatures are directly under threat from something toxic? Think about it. Does that make it go away, or does that very focus make the 'problem' even worse?

Three: What do we all agree is the most powerful force in the universe? If the answer is love, and I am suspecting it most likely is, then why are we not using that force in a circumstance such as this? Do we not really believe that? Is it just words, or just for 'good' situations, and not 'bad' ones, to add in another healthy dose of duality here?

When I trained years ago, as a psychotherapist, it was a pretty rigorous training. Eight years in all, twice weekly therapy, twice-weekly supervision, group therapy, the lot. I did not know about energy then. However, we *were* taught about a phenomenon called 'projection.' Projection is a term that describes the sending out and receiving another's thoughts, feelings, memories, experiences, fantasies, as if they are your own. The therapist's job is to work out what is not theirs, what belongs to the other person, and to use that to understand what the other is struggling to manage, tolerate, accept, allow into consciousness. Therefore, a therapist is using all their senses all the time. When I think about it, I have been unwittingly working with energy for many, many years. However, it was never presented as dangerous. We were never frightened of it. It was the stuff of everyday work in the therapy room. One of the foundations of a good therapist. Therefore, in psychotherapy training, we were not taught to fear projection; we were taught to see it as a communication. We were taught to receive it willingly, but to separate out in our psyche what was ours and what had been received from the other. Nothing fear-based, nothing threatening, just the thing that always happens when people get together. Especially when someone is 'splitting.'

Splitting. Splitting off. Another useful psychotherapy term. It means we cannot allow what we are feeling into our consciousness, so we send it out away from ourselves. That usually means that it is picked up by someone else's energy field. See - this stuff has been known about and studied and written about in learned journals and used consciously for a good 150 years, and not once was anyone even hinting that it should be something to fear.

When you see it like this, it isn't frightening, or attacking, or evil, or threatening. It doesn't need to be smudged away. I don't know any therapists whose therapy rooms smell of white sage smoke! The crucial thing is this. Because we knew about this as a phenomenon, and had been taught to expect, accept and process what we were receiving, we just got on and *did* it. Therapists are pretty good at knowing what is theirs and what is not. And whatever is not theirs, is simply an unconscious communication from someone who *does not know what they are communicating*, or even that they are communicating energetically at *all*. So now, if we think this through again, we can start to see that projection is not malevolent. The other's feelings or wishes might be, but *projection* is a communication of them, not a receiving of them. No one can create in our reality, and no one can put his or her energy into us. It is a communication only.

In the years in between, I have learned to understand energy much more, and to work with it as a reiki master. There have been a number of instances where I have known that other energy has been around. Some beautiful, some troubled. But *always*, the response required is the same: *Love*. So we most helpfully counter projection with love, not fear. We need to recognize that we have received a communication, and work out what it is. Then process it with compassion and understanding. And then, we act in whatever way we choose. My own way is to say something like, 'I have heard, Beloved. Namaste. I release this to the Universe.' And I do so with loving intention that the energy be transmuted, and the other receive whatever help is needed for their higher good. I use the word 'Beloved' because it reminds me to recognize that I am interacting with another spark of divine energy, who is a mirror of myself. It is inappropriate for me to respond in any other way. We are all unique, and we are All One.

Anyhow, that is my take on it. We do not need to develop fear; we need to develop ever-greater awareness. It is what at all the great sages - excuse the pun - have said all down the ages. Go within, do the work, know yourself so that you can process what is yours and what is another's. We are all Source energy, all divine beings of light and love, having a human experience out here on the leading edge.

Don't we all deserve this gift from one another?

Then there will be you

There will always be
The haters
The doubters
The you can'ts
The you're not allowed to people
The no one has ever people
The why would you people
The me first people
The people are this way people
The mockers
The inside the box people.

And then there'll be *you*,
proving them all *wrong!*

The shadow

It doesn't take us long, does it, to figure out that the best way to be accepted is to do our best to *hide* the unacceptable parts of ourselves, and to show only the parts which we deem to be acceptable to the world..

We learn this early on in a series of "Don't Be" statements: 'don't be angry, don't be selfish, don't be mean, don't be greedy.' We learn that to do any of these things makes us a bad person, and so we hide these parts of ourselves not only from the world, but ultimately from ourselves as well. If the world hates and despises these things, then we must surely hate and despise them too. And so we create our 'shadow side.' When people talk about their 'shadow side', it is qualities such as this that they are referring to. When Carl Jung coined this beautifully imaginative and evocative phrase, many years ago, this is what he meant: everything that we deem or perceive to be unacceptable and shameful is felt to be our 'shadow.'

In reality, of course, we all have a shadow side, and as a therapist I spend my working life helping my clients to accept and integrate what they feel is unacceptable about themselves back into their picture of themselves, to be whole. Since only when we can accept all of who we are can we be truly healthy and truly free. Here is what happens when we push everything into our 'shadow self':

We shut down emotionally; we no longer know what we feel. To dare to feel is to risk feeling bad things. We could not survive feeling bad things. Because we are out of touch with what we feel, we walk around like a coiled spring of emotion out of control. We lack awareness and so are liable to explode or collapse without warning when something triggers us into acting out the feelings we are suppressing. It also means that we can never feel good about ourselves because we spend so much time focusing on, and trying to hide, what we believe to be our bad bits.

Another consequence of pushing away all the 'bad emotion' is that we end up feeling flat and empty and hollow because we have inevitably pushed away all the 'good emotion' too.

Because we are judging ourselves so vigorously and harshly, we end up judging everyone else in the same way, and so we despise and hate in others what are actually aspects of our own shadow side. It is this we are referring to when we talk about being mirrors or reflections of each other. We deny parts of ourselves only to perceive them and despise or attack them in others. This affects and colors our view of the whole world, since we project out into the world the disavowed parts of ourselves that we are hiding from ourselves. Therefore, not only do we see those parts in others; we decide that the whole world is this way. It becomes hard to see goodness anywhere. So the world becomes a bad place full of bad people all doing bad things while pretending to be good. We blame everyone and everything else instead of taking personal responsibility, because taking personal responsibility involves accepting and admitting we are less than perfect, which is unthinkable. We are always right and everyone else is wrong because the cause of our unhappiness and discontent is 'out there'

We also fall into the trap of 'if only.' If only this, or if only that, everything would be perfect and we would be happy.

The reason for doing shadow work is to undo all this, to heal the split between what we allow of ourselves and what we deny or push away. To help us to integrate all our different split off and hidden from view bits and become whole. To help us to stop hiding from ourselves and accept all of who we are, with compassion and without judgment. To accept fully our humanity. To end our suffering from guilt and shame. And in doing so, to accept our divinity also.

As a therapist in training, exploring and integrating our shadow side was an absolutely central and essential aspect of the personal work we all had to do. There was nowhere to hide, and rightly so. It is why therapists are so comfortable talking about difficult things, and owning difficult bits of themselves. The training and the personal and group therapy is rigorous and takes you apart in order that you really know who you are. But the freedom it brings is extraordinary.

Shadow work aims to do something similar. Once we stop hiding from ourselves, we can stop hiding from the rest of the world. We can let go of the illusion that perfect exists. Instead, we can stand in the beauty of our perfect human imperfection. We did not come here to live in shame for experiencing the whole range of human emotion and experience; we came here to embrace and taste it all. Do you catch the wonder of that? We have to discover, own, accept and embrace everything we are, because that is why we came. It is our destiny to be whole; we are more than deserving. We are worthy of love, and of our own love. We have never been unlovable, ever. We are deserving of forgiveness and compassion, of understanding and unconditional acceptance. In any case, seen from this perspective, forgiveness ceases to be even necessary.

When we can say, 'I AM ' to the deepest, darkest aspect of ourselves, we are then capable of becoming all we are meant to be. We cannot see each other, or be seen, until we stop hiding. More important still, we cannot love another, unconditionally, until we, ourselves, have embraced all that *we* are as loveable. That is, we cannot fully love until we ourselves know that we are fully loveable. Every bit of us. We cannot be fully free until we can free ourselves to feel whatever we feel without judgment. And to understand just who we really are. For what we call our shadow side is necessary in order for us to appreciate the depth and breadth of our humanity and the depth and breadth of our divinity, and to allow others to do the same.

That is how big this is. That is the crux of it. We free not only ourselves when we own and acknowledge our shadow; we free everyone around us to do so as well. All pretense is gone, because it is no longer needed. Everyone is freed. And we allow healing where healing is needed. For when the shadow is transformed, it becomes Love, and compassion beyond measure. That is the path to healing and the shadow's true purpose. It is always to lead us to unconditional love. Every aspect of ourselves is a gift. Our shadow side is there to remind us that we are incomplete until we have learned love, forgiveness, kindness, tolerance, compassion. Not just for others but for ourselves. Most of all, for ourselves, for that is the most difficult challenge of all. It is at the heart of expansion. We cannot feel these emotions fully towards others *until* we can feel them towards ourselves. Judgment of self will always breed judgment of others. Love and compassion towards self will always breed love and compassion for others. It can be no other way.

Our dark side is only dark while we keep it hidden. When we bring it out into the open, we discover what an amazing and powerful gift we have unwrapped. And that deeply sacred experience always transforms us. Suddenly we are gloriously, joyfully, and forever free!

Light

Light is warmth
Light is glow
Light is clarity
Light is illumination
Light is response
Light is purpose
Light is meaning
Light is brightness
Light is unburdening
Light is relief
Light is sparkle
Light is uniqueness
Light is dispelling
Light is cleansing
Light is hope
Light is inspiration
Light is dawning
Light is all that is
Light is

Feelings are neutral

Contrary to what many of us are conditioned to believe, feelings are neutral, neither good nor bad. It is as pointless to judge yourself for experiencing a feeling, as it is to judge yourself for catching a cold. Feelings simply are. They become problematic only when they are suppressed or denied. Embraced without judgment, they are our emotional guidance system. They tell us what is going on emotionally, rather than our just relying on what is going on in our head.

When we listen only to our head, we become caught up in 'shoulds' and 'ought tos', whereas when we allow our feelings too, our rational, logical mind is balanced by our heart. Rather than suppressing, denying, or dismissing an emotion, when we allow and experience it, it changes. When we experience an emotion, we begin to process the experience that gave rise to it. Everything joins up healthily, rather than being split off or chopped up and dislocated. We cannot integrate feeling and experience while we are still judging. To integrate we must accept and allow.

We often fear what allowing ourselves to feel fully will mean. We talk about drowning, or starting to cry and not being able to stop. Actually, in reality, the opposite is true. When we allow ourselves to experience, and stay with, or go into, an emotion, it leads us towards inner peace. Think of the relief we feel after a good rant or a good cry! By accepting and allowing the truth of what we feel, by allowing our authentic self to be wrapped in a warm blanket of loving compassion, by just flowing with it, we begin to release and transform it. It is far more painful and exhausting to suppress our emotions, to struggle in the judging and condemning of them, than it is to experience them. It is the struggle to suppress our pain that really hurts, and which also prolongs it. Nothing changes when we hate, deny, or despise ourselves, or parts of ourselves. If anything, those parts becomes magnified and seem to us to grow uglier. Paradoxically, it is only when we accept ourselves as we are that we are able to change. While we judge and suppress, we are unable to move from where we are. We are too busy hiding and defending to be able to shift or evolve.

Emotions are part of our wholeness. They are a sure sign of health, not weakness or badness or pathology. By welcoming each and every emotion, we allow ourselves to grow and change. To be free to be all we are destined to be. We do not live in an emotionless universe, and we are not meant to be analytical beings, without feelings. We came here to experience it all, not just half. So why would we decide that there are things we should feel, and things we should not feel? Why would we settle for a fragment or a snippet only, when we actually came here to experience the complete package?

We are source energy, complete, whole, fully aware, curious and expanding, able to choose, accept, allow, hold everything in a state of compassion and grace. We are not here to judge, nor to be judged. We are pure love expanding through the challenges and contrasts of experiencing fully what it is to be human. We came for the experience, not to judge experience. In terms of expansion, that makes no sense. We are love and light, and we are appreciate just how gloriously unique every single experience we came here to taste and know in this physical time/space reality actually is. We came to play this delicious and intricate game, as if this is who we really are, while at the same time observing it through the eyes of the eternal and infinite consciousness we also are. Who is there to judge?

Feelings make us human, they bring us to life. They are why we came. Let go, allow, accept, and be curious. Enjoy!

Little boy in the sea

· ·

I am laying on my beach lounger, relaxing in the sun, when I become aware of a small child crying. The sound is piercing, unrelenting, and frightened. This child is really scared.

Over the top of the child's crying there comes another voice, a man's gruff, irritated voice. The man's voice is telling the child not to be so silly. To stop crying. I am curious and sit up to see what is happening. A little to my right, I see a toddler, maybe fourteen to sixteen months old, standing in the sea beside a tall, thick set man. The man is holding the toddler's hand, but it is not a tender scene. The man is determined that this child must enjoy this paddle in the sea, and is angry that his son is frightened. The man is taking his son's fear personally. It is a reflection on him as a father that his son has not yet learned to be brave.

The father is humiliated and shamed by having a toddler crying in the sea. The toddler is sobbing and begging to be picked up. He is so upset he drags his legs and hangs off the man's arm. Begging. But the man tells him he is too big to be carried and that he must stop crying and stop being such a baby. Stop being a 'cry baby.'

This toddler is not allowed to be the baby that he is. The essence that he is. He is being told that he must be strong, and not cry. He must not let the world - the world being whatever his father is casting it to be - see that he is 'weak.' He may not be real; he may not show it like it is; he must learn to feel ashamed if he allows others to see what he truly feels. And so the lessons are learned. The fear-based lessons. The ego rules lessons. The life on this earth lessons. This little boy is learning that others will be appalled, just like his father is appalled, at any display of anything other than happy, positive, life is wonderful and I'm lovin' it, kind of feeling.

This child is learning to grow a 'false self.' He is learning to pretend. From now on, life must be lived in the head, with a view to what others will think, rather than from the heart. From fear-based ego rather than from love-based essence. Life on this planet has begun, and we are teaching him the rules. We are fragile and our sensitivities are delicate. He is not allowed to shake us up, or to make us feel uncomfortable or exposed.

So let's have a think about this thing called vulnerability. This thing that this little boy is no longer allowed to show. The thing that, with time and reinforcement, he will not even remember that he ever even knew. How are *we* to think about it? Those of us who are seeing a bigger picture, who are reawakening to what this adventure we call life is all about? What are we to make of it? Well, the fear-based ego shuns vulnerability. So let us wonder why that would be. How about we start with a dictionary definition of 'vulnerable': "capable of being wounded."...."open to attack or damage."

Maybe what this definition *really* means is something like "*inability* to manage or survive wounding or attack or damage." Inability makes the world of difference. It says that to be vulnerable is to reveal that you are not able to manage difficulty. It says that vulnerability is weakness. And that means that vulnerability is shameful, and something to be hidden.

And yet, from a therapist's perspective, the thing that makes us 'weak' - capable of breaking, collapsing, being unable to negotiate the challenges of life, finding it hard to recover from emotionally difficult experiences - is precisely the rigidity and inflexibility which this father is teaching his child. It is exactly the inability to feel, or face feelings, which creates weakness in the psyche. Plasticity and flexibility make us strong. Allowing ourselves to be vulnerable makes us strong. The qualities that build resilience - the ability to embrace all that happens to us in life and *not* break - are all about not living in the head. They are about being aware, being able to recognize what we are feeling and express it appropriately. They are about openness, emotional and psychological honesty, self-awareness and reflectivity.

And you cannot do *any* of these things if you are having to pretend all the time. Because if you are pretending to the rest of the world you will not know true intimacy, and if you are pretending to the rest of the world you will end up pretending even to yourself. You will not even *know* you anymore. You will know who you *think* you are, you will know who you *ought* to be. But you will *not* know who you *really* are. And *that* is what is frightening. Not someone noticing that you are crying because you are feeling scared. It is when we do not *know* what we are feeling; when we do not *know* we are feeling tender or fragile, that we break. *Not* when we are feeling those things but can acknowledge and accept and allow them. When we do that, we grow through the experience, and we are stronger for it.

It is when we don't have the battle going on between what we are feeling somewhere deep down, and what we believe we *ought* to be feeling, that we are simply free to be joined up, to be ourselves, to breathe and laugh and cry and just *be*. We do not have to wear so-called 'strength' as some kind of badge of honor. It really is not. Truly. It is pretend living. It is half living. It is a divided, false-self kind of living. It is numb, tuned out turned down living. It is not what we came here to do. Not at all. It is living from the ego. It is not living from the heart.

Now, I can hear some voices telling me I have got this all wrong. What about the whole issue of energy and vibration, for instance? What about all that stuff about not 'beating the drum' of negative stuff? I can see how this could sound like the absolute opposite of what leading edge spirituality, grounded in the laws of quantum physics and vibration, is saying. Actually, there is not in conflict at all. No one is saying beat the drum of fear and pain and misery. No one is saying do not think about the importance of vibration and alignment. No one, certainly, is saying *stay* in that place longer than you have to. However, what I *am* suggesting is that we can only make a choice about our emotional energy when we actually *know* what that emotional energy *is*. And that means *going* there first.

A wonderful therapist, Daniel Segal, who works from a place of being both mindful himself as a therapist, and of teaching and encouraging clients to be mindful too, talks about what he calls the 'spiritual by-pass.' By this, he means the way that so many of us think that we can conduct a simple by-pass operation, where we can avoid dealing with all the things that have caused us contrast, or emotional upset, and jump straight to pure invulnerable positivity. He would maintain, as would I, that it is not avoidance, but integration, which is the key to spiritual strength and well-being. From the place of integration - that is, knowing, accepting, understanding and allowing our shadow side and all the contrast it has brought us - we facilitate true and lasting expansion. It is then that we are no longer wobbly, no longer susceptible to breaking or collapsing. When we have done the work. And the spiritual path, let no one tell you differently, involves work.

It is so easy to believe, quite simplistically, that you simply decide what to feel and you feel it. In fact, it is often put over that way. Or maybe that is just how we receive it, because we want to. What is said less obviously, but is nevertheless understood very well by every enlightened spiritual teacher I have ever come across, is that, unless we are *aware* of what we feel, unless we can read our emotional guidance system well, we cannot make a change or a choice at a *feeling* level. And that is the only way it can be effective. We have to know what we really feel before we can decide to change that feeling by changing our emotional response. Otherwise, we are flailing around in the dark.

That is, we must be real first. We must have become able to see beyond the ego, beyond the fear that it generates, to where the heart is, and the love that it generates. Anything less, however hard you try, and however badly you want it, and no matter what affirmations you keep on making, will not cut it. Your vibration will be that of the ego, rather than of your essence. And that will lower your vibration again and again. And you will wonder why things are not going the way you are wanting them to.

So back to vulnerability, and the importance of this much maligned quality. And back to our perception of what vulnerability actually is. From an ego-based perspective, to show that we are vulnerable, in any way, is to give others the opportunity to see our weakness, the bits of us that leave us open to attack, or to mockery, or for what we reveal to be used against us. But how about from the perspective we hold when we are in touch with the essence that we actually are? Well, then we see a quite different reality. We see that to feel, to be open, to show our humanity, is to acknowledge our oneness. To fully recognize each other as the source energy we are. To fully *be*.

It means saying it like it is and not worrying if it gives something away about who we are. Because being who we are is exactly why we came. We came to share and experience our uniqueness. And so, it means showing up and being real, understanding that to not do so is to deny others, to deny the universe, what we came here to be and to share.

It means being willing to show up when another is allowing their vulnerability to be seen and showing them that it is okay. It also means really wanting to know the true answer when we say, 'How are you?' rather than wanting to hear the politically correct version, which is, 'I'm really great!' It means throwing out the pretense of the false self and showing up *as you are*. It means not leaving another alone because you cannot bear any answer other than, 'Wonderful!' That does not mean, as the ego fears, that everyone will suddenly start moaning and whinging and becoming negative, pulling you down. It actually means that people will be free to express the full range of their humanity. Not just the acceptable bits. All of it. The joy and the pain, the anger and the love, all of it. Fully. Without apology. As Source. We are in true alignment when we are acting from our essence, our higher self, who we really are. And that essence is love-based, not fear-based. And to act from a base of love is to allow vulnerability. Not to allow another's vulnerability and not your own, however; but to dare to be vulnerable in return. Far from being weakness, that is courage and bravery without limit.

So our little boy in the sea was actually being who he really was. He was in touch with his essence, and just saying it like it was. All he needed was for his father to allow that vulnerability and be vulnerable back. To pick him up and give him a hug. To listen and really hear. To let go of his shame and stop letting others define him. To stand up and be counted. To show his son who he really was. Is that not why we came? Is that not what we are here to do? Is that not what oneness is about! The recognition that we are *All That Is?* That *all* is acceptable, *all* is significant, *all* is sacred and of use? That *all* is expansion? Is that not what being spiritually focused, being mindful, really is?

So every time you reach for what is real, and are allowing yourself to be vulnerable, you have taken the courageous decision to be *you* as you *are* And that will bring you home. Always. Your intuition, your inner beingness, will tell you. Alignment is not about being constantly cheery and effervescently upbeat. It is about being in touch with the Love that you are, and that we all are. Sometimes it feels ecstatic, joyous; sometimes it is peaceful and quietly content. It is all good. That is when we manifest what we want, when we witness miracles, when everything falls into place. When the magic happens.

So next time you're tempted to say the thing you've been conditioned to believe you *ought* to say, or to pretend you're feeling one thing when you're really feeling another, maybe it's worth a quick inner dialogue....... Fear or Love. Where do you stand?

Heidi

· ·

Time for another fairy tale...

This story is about a little girl called Heidi.

She might just as easily have been called Lizzie, or Suzie, or she could have been a little boy called Johnny, or Matthew. However, in our story, right now, she is called Heidi.

Are you sitting comfortably? Then I will begin...

There was once a little girl called Heidi. She was a very lucky little girl, because when she was born she was a very beautiful baby, and so everyone fell in love with her. The midwives who helped deliver her, the nurses on the ward, the other visitors, her mummy and daddy. Most of all, her mummy and daddy. Her mummy and daddy were so proud of Heidi they could not wait to show her off. They were just so excited at what they had managed to produce. She was so, so perfect, and they loved her because she was so perfect.

As Heidi grew up, she became ever more beautiful. Friends of her mummy would tell her that they could eat her, and friends of her daddy told her she would break many hearts one day. Heidi did not really like the idea of breaking people's hearts, and pondered on that a great deal. She did not feel too comfortable about being eaten, either. It felt somehow sort of like being gobbled up like a bowl of jelly and ice cream. It just felt a bit weird inside, not quite safe. Yes, not quite safe.

As Heidi grew up, her mummy and daddy spared no expense. They dressed her up in the most gorgeous, cutest, prettiest clothes and shoes, grew her hair really long so they could put it into lots of different styles for different looks and different occasions, brought sweet jewelry to go with her outfits, and told her she looked like a princess. Heidi sometimes found it a bit hard to keep up the excitement at all these new and wonderful things. She knew it was ungrateful not to love them, and that it was letting her mummy and daddy down if she did not do all the twirls, and pose, smiling, for all the photos they and all her relatives wanted to take.

To tell the truth, she was a bit alarmed when men she did not really know would come up and squeeze her cheeks, or blow kisses at her and wink. Once, a man raised her hand to his lips to kiss it, and then fell on the floor clutching his heart. She felt frightened because she thought he was dying, and could not understand why her mummy and daddy were laughing. Heidi knew that it was very important to her mummy and daddy that she was beautiful, and that everyone loved her. She became very good at producing a smile on demand, and at saying things she knew other people would find cute and loveable. She knew how very important it was to be loveable.

Then, one day, Heidi discovered that she had grown up. She knew she would be okay in this grown up world because she knew how to dress beautifully, to be charming, to demonstrate nice manners, to say things that people would find loveable.

Then, bit by bit, life started to get a bit more complicated. The things that she had always found worked, the things that made her loveable, did not always seem to be working any more. And she realized, with a huge pang of fear, that there were things she did not know how to do. It was suddenly really frightening. It did not seem to be enough to be beautiful. It did not make people love her. People said things like she was 'shallow' and 'empty-headed' and 'false.' And the most frightening thing of all was that she had absolutely no idea whatsoever what on earth they were talking about. There *were* people who still seemed to find her lovable. And beautiful. A certain kind of man, men who wanted her in a certain way. They reminded her of the way the men who used to squeeze her cheeks when she was a little girl used to look at her. But although they said they loved her, they never behaved as if they did after a while, even though she would smile and say nice things, just as if she had been taught.

Heidi was bewildered, and frightened, and deeply miserable. Somewhere, deep down, she too knew that she was 'shallow.' She understood enough of what people meant when they used that word to know that they were right. It meant there was not enough to her. That she was not enough. It meant she pretended a lot, did and said what she thought people wanted her to do and say, and that if ever she tried to think what she herself thought or felt she could not find out. It was not there. There was nothing there.

This was getting really terrifying...there was nothing there!

Suddenly, Heidi found herself running. She found she could not run fast enough, or far enough, in her heels, so she pulled them off one at a time and ran barefoot instead. And suddenly, the busy street she had been running along in her high heels faded away, seemed to merge into something else, and she realized that she was running barefoot on grass. And then the light seemed to fade, the world grew dimmer, and she was running through trees, denser and denser, until she found herself in the middle of a forest. She allowed herself to slow to a walk, and began picking her way more carefully through the undergrowth. Finally, she sat herself down on a fallen tree trunk, put her face in her hands, and sobbed and sobbed. She sobbed as if she would never stop, loud desperate sobs, the built up over a whole lifetime kind of sobs. She thought she would never be all cried out.

But when at last the sobbing began to ease, and turned finally to caught breaths and sniffles, she was surprised to see, on looking up, a man sitting on a boulder opposite her, with his back against a tree.

She was startled to see him, and half made to get up and run some more, but there was something in the gentle gesture of his hand, raised slightly in a soothing wave, that said, 'please stay,' and the warmth of deep kindness and concern in his eyes, as they held hers, that made her sit down again. Heidi was aware of a strange stillness, a peacefulness, a sense that it was safe here. She looked at the man, old and bearded, dressed in a long plain garment, belted at the waist with rope. She could sense his kindness, his patience, his steadiness. He was not like any man she had ever met before. He was wise, knowing.

'So.' The wise old man spoke.

He seemed to be waiting for her to speak. She had no idea what he wanted her to say. She was used to knowing what people wanted her to say. But this was not like that. 'I don't know what you want me to say,' she eventually murmured. The wise old man nodded, slowly, and clearly understood. He nodded again, and waited. Heidi knew that there was nothing to be rushed here.

She looked at him and his eyes held hers. It was such a strange feeling, a first-ever-felt feeling, as if he could see right into her. She felt the terror grip suddenly - she had forgotten for one moment the awful truth. But he would see. He would know. Just like everyone else, he would see that there was nothing there. When he looked inside, he would see.

'Don't look at me,' she burst out. 'You mustn't look at me!' The old man looked at the ground briefly. She sensed he had no wish to shame her or make her feel stupid. But when he looked back up, she was shocked to see that there were tears glistening in his eyes. She did not understand. Why would he be in tears? What had she said to upset him? Had she hurt his feelings?

The old man smiled at her, and then spoke. 'My child,' he said. (Heidi was puzzled - why had he called her that?) Again, he said, 'My child.' It was a mixture of recognition and sorrow...'don't you know who you are?'

It was such a strange question, so totally not expected. Why would he ask her that? Of-course she knew who she was. She started to tell him, but he held up his hand again, laid his fingers against his lips. And then he met her eyes and held them, for so long that she found herself holding her breath from the intensity of it, before he said, quietly, 'I mean, don't you know who you *really* are?' 'Would you like me to show you?' 'I think so...' Heidi breathed.

She knew this was huge, momentous, a little scary, but really important.

From the pocket of his gown, the old man drew out a mirror. He offered it to her. She hesitated for a moment - she had looked in so many mirrors - but then she took it. She looked at herself, her face grubby, her hair a mess, her dress a bit torn, from running through the forest. 'I look terrible.' she said. The old man looked very serious, earnest. 'May I hold the mirror for you?' he asked. She handed it to him, and he did a strange thing. He took a deep breath, and then breathed onto the mirror. Actually, it seemed more like *into* the mirror, because his breath had somehow disturbed the mirror's surface. As he held it, and she looked, the mist began to clear, and what she saw made her gasp. She shot a look at the old man, and saw that his expression was steady and grave. He nodded encouragement, and she looked back into the mirror.

The face which looked back at her was extraordinarily beautiful. It was radiant, incandescent, and translucent almost. It was composed of almost blinding white light, shimmering and sparkling. It was utterly, breathtakingly beautiful. She looked at the gentle old man for explanation, but instead he pulled from behind the tree a longer, taller mirror. He signaled her to wait where she was, still holding her hand mirror, as he came to stand behind her, and positioned the taller mirror at such an angle that she could see into it through her own mirror.

'Now look,' he whispered.

In the mirror, Heidi saw, going on and on and on, for as far back as she could see, other beings, just like the reflection she had seen in her mirror. Each one was looking at her, and smiling, as if they knew her. Like she was known and precious to them. And as she looked, she felt the most amazing heat, like a blanket surrounding her. It was like having countless loving arms wrapped around her. She wanted to say so much. She wanted to say that she did not feel hollow any more. And that she did not feel like she was not enough anymore. There was so much she wanted to say to this strange, kindly old man who had shown her this. She turned to tell him, to try to find the words, but she could not see him.

Then, as she looked back into the mirror, she saw him, right at the back, no longer wearing the old robe and long beard, but glistening and sparkling like sunshine on water, radiating light over them all. As she watched, the mirror misted over, and became solid once more, and she was alone in the forest.

She sat for a very long time. It was almost dusk when she decided she would go back. She felt bereft of the old man who had shown her such kindness and wonders, but she no longer felt empty or hollow. Instead, she felt a certainty and depth, almost a sense of meaning, she had never known before.

As she got up to leave, she heard the tinkling of bells, and the wind whispered in her ear, 'Always remember.'

And she always did.

The bridge

· ·

We are all
looking on
from the bridge.
There is no 'other'
no 'somewhere else'
no 'someone else.'
Nothing is
as it seems.
There is only
'now' and 'here'
and 'we.'
Let that
be enough,
and in this moment,
say, 'Let it be, let it be.'
We are all
just a breath away.
a heartbeat.
One heartbeat.
The One Heartbeat.
Let it be, let it be.

On fear

I wonder what the most basic human fear is. If there is such a thing? Fear of rejection? Fear of humiliation? Fear of failure? Fear of success? Fear of being powerless? Too powerful? All-powerful?

Fear of commitment, of being trapped, controlled? Fear of caring, loving, being hurt, being loved, or unloved? Fear of loneliness, fear of loss? Fear of making mistakes, of thinking for ourselves? Fear of change, fear of freedom? Fear of responsibility? Fear of our emotions, of feeling, being vulnerable at the hands of our emotions? Of getting angry, upset? Of losing it? Fear of fear itself?

So what is fear about? At its most fundamental, what is fear really about? I think it has a great deal to do with feeling unsafe. That the ground beneath our feet is not solid and can fall away at any moment. And what is it that drives that sense of being unsafe? It is that, in that moment, we feel completely alone. That there is no help, no presence looking on, and no witness. We are utterly alone. That means not just physically, but emotionally and psychically alone. The experience that, if you are a young baby, can lead to you ceasing to thrive, or to even lose the will to live.

One of the essential experiences, developmentally, for an infant, is what we therapist's call 'being alone in the presence of another,' Imagine a toddler, absorbed in play, sitting on the floor caught up in the wonderful imaginary world the toddler is creating. Picture this toddler feeling totally secure in the knowledge that a kindly and tuned in adult is sitting nearby, constantly aware, watching and keeping them safe. This is a secure aloneness, which carries a deep awareness of maintained connection. There is no sense of separation. All is well.

The aloneness I am referring to is not the same as solitude. Solitude is possible because there is a knowledge of our connection to all things, even though we are physically on our own. Solitude carries no threat, unless we fear finding the sense of aloneness within that experience, and then the experience of solitude plunges us into a terrible chasm or void we can come to fear so much. The sense of aloneness that fuels fear is based on the belief that we are utterly separate, completely alone, without help or care, in a reality where that is true of everyone else too. If we know we are not alone, we know we are safe. If we feel we are alone, utterly existentially alone, then we cannot possibly feel safe. So fear is about feeling utterly on our own, vulnerable, without help, and – crucially - separate from everyone and everything else. At times when it hits really severely, the word terror would be more accurate. Try it out, see if that feels right. Fear always involves the sense of being unsafe and separate.

So how do we manage fear? Well, besides pushing on through it, rather than being paralyzed by it - making ourselves push on through fight or flight rather than going into freeze – if fear is about feeling utterly *alone* and *separated* from everything else, then the solution must always be to remember that we are all *One*. That separateness is an illusion only, that we are all aspects of a greater whole. That we are never alone, even when we feel alone. And that we are at all times surrounded by more love and light than we can possibly begin to comprehend from this human perspective.

And at the same time, it is to remember that this greater whole is loving, compassionate, trustworthy, reliable, and infinitely good, beyond our wildest imagining. And that not only are we part of this whole, we also are that whole, as is everything else. Therefore, we never can be alone, ever. We can feel as if we are alone, but we can never actually be alone. We are surrounded by, and in intimate communication with, so much loving, supportive, powerful energy, whose sole purpose is to guide us and help us to remember that never, even for just a moment, are we ever alone. This means that we are known, recognized, delighted in, loved. And that we have always been known, recognized, delighted in, and loved. And that we always will be.

There is nowhere we can ever be where this is not so. Nowhere. Nothing else and nowhere else exists.

When we really get hold of this, truly grasp it, we see that all there is, beyond the illusion of separateness, is oneness. And once we allow that, then we begin to allow all that is loving and abundant into our awareness and we begin to live our lives from that glorious perspective. A wise soul once said, 'Fear is just pulling a face at yourself in the mirror.' That is, it is seeing the wrong face in the mirror, the illusion rather than the reality. Once you step through the illusion in the mirror, and comprehend that what you thought you saw was not real, not accurate, not how it truly is, you free yourself to see instead the magnificent being of light and love, the powerful creator, infinite and eternal source of wisdom and compassion, ever expanding, which you actually are. As am I. As are we all.

The truth is that you have the entire universe inside you, just as we all do. We are the creator of worlds and infinite parallel realities, you are a version of me, I am a version of you, and we are all profoundly and intimately One. We are a part, and we are also the whole. Therefore, in oneness, you are never alone. When you ask, the universe responds, because the universe vibrates in time to you. And we all resonate with each other. What is happening to one is felt and known by all. Can you feel that? Do you get what that means?

Fully take that in. The comfort of it, the strength of it, the power of it. Then know, without any shadow of a doubt, that love, not fear, is who you are. And step into the magic of that!

We are the dream catchers

We are the dream catchers,
the spinners of the web,
the visionaries,
the lightbearers,
the old ones,
the wise ones,
the sparkly ones,
the magical ones,
the ones who see,
the ones who remember,
who have always been
and will always be.
We are made of stars
and we dance among them,
as our laughter and songs
are carried on the wind
to the furthest corners
of the Universe.
We are all and none and the space between,
an ocean of light and love
of the highest and purest vibration,
Source energy, liquid love,
Flowing for all eternity.

On loving

I reckon that one of the things we find hardest of all to do is to love. I think it is one of our greatest challenges, and greatest frustrations. And the cause of some of our deepest wounds. I realize that I could be accused of making a sweeping generalization here. You could say so easily that this is simply not true. That of-course we know how to love. We love our children, our families, our pets, our friends...what on earth do I mean? Who do I think I am to say such a thing!

If we really knew how to love, deeply, unconditionally, with true kindness and compassion, without expecting something in return, so much suffering would cease overnight. The truth is that, where love, unconditional love, is concerned, we so easily and readily pull right back, allow fear to take over, and retreat from each other. Individually and on a global scale. In order to love unconditionally we have to face some unpalatable truths. We have to unlearn the 'lessons' of a lifetime, all lodged deep within the dark places of our fear-based unconscious mind.

People often come to see me asking why they can't seem to achieve a place of happiness, of being at peace, of trusting that all will be well, of forgiving and letting go, of loving unconditionally in the way they want to. They feel like they get there for a while, and then suddenly they find themselves in a place of despair, or grief, or rage, or deep mistrust, a place of feeling vulnerable, frightened of being hurt again, that the world is an unsafe place. They work hard to use affirmations, they read inspirational books, they listen to spiritual teachers and try hard to do what they say is helpful, is right. Yet none of these, although they can help, has proved to be life transforming in the way they hoped.

And I suggest they are seeing through the filter of *past* experience, through the eyes of the child they were, through the old familiar patterns of relationships they have known. That these, although passed and gone, have left their emotional and psychological footprints and that, until those footprints are rubbed out, they will continue to trample through their unconscious, and they will surface intermittently in their conscious mind to disturb and confuse and spoil *now*. That is not just so much psychobabble. It is how the energy of all this works.

I suggest that, instead of feeling that this must all be ignored as if it didn't happen, it can effectively be healed by viewing those events - and the child/past self who experienced them - with compassion, kindness, forgiveness. By changing the energy associated with those memories and the associations they carry, and which emit a vibration incompatible with the unconditional love either of our own self or of another. And I witness a weight lift as they take the child/past self that they were, vulnerable, innocent and unknowing, and instead of regarding that self with shame, humiliation, repulsion, embrace it with love, understanding, and admiration. And as the weight lifts, grace, ease, peace and joy flood in. And love. Most of all, Love.

For it is only when we have learned to feel compassion, kindness, forgiveness for ourselves, when we have forgiven the perceived failures, imperfections, weaknesses of the past or present - for they *are* perceptions only - only then can we love ourselves unconditionally. We have to remove judgment from ourselves - for that is part of the fear that is lurking: if this is how we feel about ourselves, see ourselves, treat ourselves, then how much more even than that will others judge us, see us, treat us. It is only when we remove such judgment and replace it with compassion that we are we free to love deeply and unconditionally, universally, profoundly, compassionately, and to forgive.

What a gift that is when we give it to ourselves. What wonderful knock on effects it has, in our hearts and minds, in our lives, in the lives of those close to us, in the world that we inhabit. How wonderful and delicious it feels to taste the freedom of it! And vibrationally, it reaches out and touches every soul, every life, on the entire planet and beyond, intimately and profoundly, with its miraculous energy.

Beauty

When I
immerse myself
in beauty,
beauty speaks back
to me.
Just as I see beauty,
I know that beauty
is seeing me.
For beauty
appreciates beauty.
Beauty rejoices
in the company
and fellowship
of beauty.
The heart expands
and the soul
sighs the deepest sigh.
Beauty has brought me
back to myself.
And in that moment
all is One.

On feeling lovable

We are so often told, in certain circles, and by certain charismatic speakers and thinkers, that we have everything we need because all we need is love, and everyone has an unlimited supply of that. Have you heard that? Do you believe it?

Sometimes it isn't as easy as that, is it? We might know it in our head, we might agree in principle. We hear other people saying this stuff as if it is the easiest thing in the world to settle down into, but we do not *feel* it. And so, at such times, while it may clearly be true for other people, it doesn't feel true for us. And that can be a pretty lonely, miserable, and confusing place to find ourselves in. The reason is simple, though not too obvious in the moment: while at any given time we may not *feel* love, it is always there, and the way we remind ourselves that it is there, and get the feeling of it back, is to give it away to others.

In the thick of it, when we are feeling anything but generous or loving, still less loveable, this nearly always seems counter-intuitive. And that is what makes it feel like there is not enough love, that there is not enough to go round. We find ourselves believing that, if you give what little love there seems to be away, then there will be even less love available for you. This is always the illusion that clients who feel unloved and unlovable, needy and hungry, are always caught up in: that there is a finite supply of love, and usually it feels like even that tiny supply is running out. How can there possibly be enough, still less an endless supply? And so there is rivalry, envy, a sense that love must be competed for, that they must jostle for position in order to get even a little of what little there is.

We therapists tend to talk about a thing called "regression" a fair bit. It means finding ourselves in a very young memory place, a very primitive place where we find ourselves re-experiencing whatever pain and fear and unhappiness, and lack, we knew when we were very little. Perceived or actual, it makes no difference to our experience when we hit what is for us a very real memory place. Regression is never a happy place; that is not how trauma memory works. Such memory is so powerful that when it is re-triggered it feels like it is happening all over again. The body, the keeper of those events and feelings we have had to push out of our conscious mind, in order to survive an experience that our young resources could not manage, stores it all as cellular memory. That *same* cellular memory is then recalled and made live again whenever something that is happening now is sufficiently similar to how it was *back then* to trigger that particular set of young feelings and responses *all over again*. That is why, when we hit those difficult times, we feel so very young, fragile, and powerless, and feel that we have so few resources to call upon. And in those very young places, our perception, our immediate and current experience of reality, was *always* one of fearful aloneness and lack.

Trouble is, if we do not know about regression, and so do not realize how easily and how often the past can be triggered in the present, we find ourselves believing a memory *as if* it is true *now*. And so we revert to a place where we simply cannot feel love, because we believe we need way more than it feels is available. We therefore find ourselves caught in a cycle of lack and fear and aloneness, and we are separated from all that is free flowing, abundant, and readily available to us if only we could find a way to allow it.

When we manage to catch ourselves out in this trick of the ego, and realize that we are aligning ourselves with memory, and with lack, and operating from fear rather than as the essence of love and abundance we really are, the mists clear and we can see again. More importantly, we can feel again. When we give our attention to simply loving, we feel enormous relief, and a movement outward. There is no longer a limited supply. Once the channels are open again, we find that we are able and eager to give love and support, in oneness and compassion, to whatever is showing up. We shift from shut down and blocked to open and flowing.

And *that* is the secret. That is what gets us right back into the divine flow of a loving universe, where we know only abundance and wellbeing. Giving love and attention to whatever is happening right now, in the moment, always gets us to exactly where we need to be, and then our entire experience of the world, and others, changes. Life becomes bountiful and supportive and no longer feels lonely and full of lack. The kindness and compassion which you find flowing from you actually creates a kind and loving world, not only for you, but for others, too. What you give out you find reflected back. The world no longer feels a cruel place.

Once you realize that this is the secret, you have made an amazing discovery. Moreover, you need never find yourself believing the ego, or memory and regression, with its emphasis on fear and lack, or find yourself trapped in a memory place, again. All you need is love – and to love – in order to find your way back, and then you remember that there is always more than enough love to go round!

You are a once only

. . . .

You are a once only
There never has been
and there never will be
another you
in all the universe
in all eternity
Thousands have paved
the way in preparation
for your arrival
at this time and in this place
and the ripples
of the energy that you are
will reach more lives
than you can possibly imagine.
Do you get it yet?
How special you are?

Earth's playground

How about we stop believing we are victims? Supposing we stop thinking that we are being punished when apparently 'bad' things happen. How about we allow ourselves to take on board what is actually happening? Allow a new spiritual perspective, grounded in the wisdom and insights of the past, but also in the cutting edge science of this quantum world we now inhabit? What would that look like?

Well, for a start, instead of seeing life as something in which fate simply deals us a random hand, or in which the Divine sets us a series of challenges and tests, which we must negotiate satisfactorily before we can home, we would see the Earth as our playground. We would say that we have chosen to be here. That, at a soul level, we have decided that it would be fun. And that, while we were about it, we would like to learn some new things that would contribute to the expansion of all that is. We would say that Source is continually expanding and evolving, and that this is through the experiencing and observing of the realities that we are going to create.

We would say that we understand that we are all beings of light and energy, and that this is the substance of the entire universe. We would understand that this is also a vibrational universe, and that its highest vibration is that of love. We would know that everything is constantly vibrating, and that vibrationally like attracts like. We would understand that matter is compressed light, and that spirit is light which is not compressed. We would understand, however, that there is no separation, and that we are all the same energy, light emerging and re-emerging.

That we have always been so and will always be so. That birth and death are just aspects of that energy emerging and re-emerging.

What an adventure, we will have thought, to inhabit a physical universe, to have a human experience, and to explore consciousness in physical form! To enjoy physicality and the experience of this life fully. To know that every experience we ever have is Source expanding through us and in us. That we can never get it wrong, we can only grow in love, wisdom, and compassion. And we would also understand why we do not remember these things, but have to rediscover them: what an amazingly creative thought, we would say to ourselves! For a while, to forget that we are magnificent beings of light and immense power, sparks of Source energy, all One. Instead, allow voluntary amnesia, and pretend for a while to be separate beings, in reality existing within a holographic universe, but seemingly existing according to the illusions of time and space.

By giving ourselves this playground, we would understand that this is how we get to explore our own uniqueness, our creative potential, our capacity for love and compassion, empathy and understanding, but also for hate, anger, envy, rivalry, destructiveness. In this make believe world, we would allow that we can create the illusion of duality, and experience fear, darkness, doubt, evil. And we can play a game in which we gradually relearn our own light, power, and connection, and remember who we are. And as we do so, expand all that is. And most importantly, in the experiencing and perceiving of all this, the nature of that expansion is to grow in love and understanding, compassion, acceptance and wisdom.

We would understand that we may choose to experience any aspect of this physical experience, including poverty, cruelty, disease, and disability, grief, alongside the wonderfully loving and joyful aspects of life. And that we will do so in the company of other sparks of Source with whom we agree to reincarnate again and again. Our soul family, or soul tribe. We would know that we can also choose 'themes' which will run through particular lifetimes, which will lead us into a deeper understanding and appreciation of intimacy, love, forgiveness, freedom, oneness. We will understand that we prepare the drama ready for its unfolding, prior to incarnating, and set the scene, agree the actors and what role they will play. And once we are ready, we jump right in, excitedly and in anticipation, and we are born and it begins!

And we would also know that, when we do choose to incarnate, we come surrounded by so many beings of light, all of whom have known us from the beginning, who have always loved us and always watched over and guided us. We are never ever alone. Never ever without guidance or help. Because that, too, is planned and agreed. And we have all the learning and wisdom of Source available to us whenever we seek it.

And if we can remember that, lots of things get easier. We do not blame, we do not point the finger, we do not judge. We do not complain, we do not feel sorry for ourselves, we do not say, 'Why me?' Because we know we chose it, and agreed it, as did everyone else we come across. We all agreed it, and planned the key events beforehand. And no matter how it seems, in this particular playground, and this particular lifetime, we are all the best of friends.

Because we are all Source, all sparks of that same energy, and therefore we are all *love*. It can be no other way. And so instead of blaming, we say,' What did you come, generously and willingly, to teach me?' Or, 'What am I meant to help you to experience/learn?' Or 'You are a mirror for me, thank you for reflecting this back to me.' Even 'It must have been so hard to be willing to agree to cause me this degree of emotional pain for my own learning. I appreciate what a sacrifice that will have been for you.' Or 'My walking away is part of my journey, and part of yours also. Peace and light'

What a difference that comprehension makes. There are no victims, only willing co-creators. Nothing is ever going wrong, and nothing is ever out of control. We are always exactly where we need to be, both for ourselves, and also in relation to everyone and everything else in this ever-expanding web we are weaving. And that web is composed of love and of light. It is pure loving energy, consciousness, awareness expanding and vibrating, holding us all in the most tender, loving, compassionate embrace. The greater part of who we are is always guiding, sharing, and supporting us. And its nature is *Love*.

Always and only *Love*. What can there possibly be to fear?

Go beyond

Go beyond
these thoughts.
They are not *You*.
Go beyond
this place.
It is not where
You are.
Go beyond
this time.
It is not where
You belong.
Become who
You are.
The Awareness
that is
living all this
through
You!

Love is who we are

· ·

I love the outcome of the experiment which was conducted on a group of boys from an apparently 'primitive' tribe, and which puts the values of so much of the so-called 'civilized' world to shame.

The boys were invited to race forward to get a reward, a prize, which could be theirs as long as they beat everyone else by getting to it first. The boys were genuinely puzzled, and could not be persuaded to take part. The researchers were surprised and, after several further unsuccessful attempts to persuade them to race forever more tempting and desirable prizes, asked them what was the matter. The boys answered, 'How can any of us be happy if we have something but our friends have had to go without. We would rather not have anything, than to leave some of us without what the others have.'

It struck me, when I first heard about this, that the people of this tribe were so much closer to living in the true awareness of who we really are, than are so very many of us in the 'civilized' world. We have been taught to rate money, possessions, things, more than love. We have been taught that we are separate from other people, with whom we are in direct competition, and who will get one over on us and take from us if they possibly can. A cutthroat world. A crazy world.

Love is who we really are, and this truth is lodged deep in our memory and awareness, always calling us back. We never quite lose that remembering. We also sense and recognize when it is not there; when we have lost it. Always, we experience a jarring sense that something is not quite right, when we find ourselves existing in that other parallel world. Love is not material things, nor is it status. It is energy. Powerful energy. The most powerful energy that exists. We recognize it and experience it as kindness, compassion, giving, joy, peace, acceptance, non-judgment, cooperation, intimacy and connectedness. It is unmistakable.

I am reminded of another tribe in which, when one of its number has committed some kind of wrongdoing or hurt, deal with that situation so very differently to the way we do. They sit in a circle around that person, and tell them, remind them and each other, of all the wonderful positive qualities they possess, all the things they have done in kindness, everything affirming they can think of. It would be so easy to be cynical about this, but that would be to respond from a place of fear. These people understand what love is, and what oneness is. They restore instead of exclude. They do this for two entire days. Can you imagine?

How wonderful it is that increasing numbers of us are beginning to awaken, and to see the world as they see it. That we are seeing a returning home to the consciousness we truly are. I have no doubt whatsoever that the next stage of evolution on this planet will be the spiritual one, and that this is the reason that you and me, and all of us who are awakening at this time, chose this moment to incarnate. It strikes me that this is what a miracle is: a cutting through the illusion of separateness and of lack, with its low vibration, and instead, a breaking through of the high vibrational energy of love. That energy, once unleashed, is unstoppable, and creates a place where anything and everything is possible. Anything and everything. All things.

How delicious and exciting that we are right here, right now, and are the vehicle through which miracles are going to happen on this planet and in the universe in our lifetime. And sincere appreciation to each and every one of us that we kept our promise and showed up!

What a ride this is going to be!

Your path

It's your path.
You decided it,
you are creating it,
choosing it,
every single moment.
You are expanding,
discovering,
tasting,
trying out,
just for the experience,
the sheer joy of it.
The fun of it.
The sheer hell of it.
And we are all
keeping you company.
Always.
Every one of us.
Thank you
for the amazing ride.
It has been
glorious!

Parents can be tricky

· ·

A great many parents are wonderful. Kind, supportive, understanding, great role models. It is not these that I am talking about when I say that parents can be tricky. I am talking specifically about parents who seem to have let us down, got it wrong, been the source of pain or fear or threat, or who have abandoned, shamed, humiliated or criticized us and taken away our joy.

Many of us struggle to get past this, don't we? It is really hard to forgive or forget hurt that happens in childhood. Hurt suffered in childhood is extreme and goes deep, and I am at no point suggesting that it is ok for children to suffer at the hands of adults. Ever. Our inner child, the child we were, needs to be heard and understood with compassion, not told to get over it, let it go. That is beyond a child to do. However, what about when we are adults, have grown up, and we want to get past what happened, move on, leave it behind us? As adults, spiritually we know it is healthier for us to let go and move forward. And as spiritual adults, we know that we must take responsibility for our own journey, and not keep blaming someone else for our struggles or difficulties. And so we try. But it is easier said than done.

The *pain* gets in the way.

But what if we are maybe starting at the wrong point? What if, before we can forgive, or forget, we must understand? What if it is not nearly as simple, this story we tell and retell, as at first it seems? Supposing we chose it all? Suppose none of it was random, or accidental? Suppose our parents were willing - even if reluctantly willing, at times - players of roles we ourselves allocated to them? That we discussed and planned it all before we all incarnated, and that the purpose was not in fact pain, but rather growth and evolution and learning? We are often willing to allow that there are no accidents in life, that there are only synchronicities. So, what if our parents were one of the biggest and most significant of all?

So why would we go to these lengths to set all this up? Let us think of some of the reasons we might choose the parents and experiences we did. This is not at all comprehensive as a list of possibilities. It is more a starting point, a few suggestions only. However, they demonstrate the general principle. I am referring to parents, since that is where the greatest sticking point seems to be for many of us. But of-course, you could substitute ex-partner, brother, sister, daughter, son, friend. Anyone who has played a major part in the experience of your life.

Maybe we choose our parents for their good qualities. We know what we need to experience that is nurturing and expanding, and we choose our parents from amongst our soul group because are willing to display those for us, so that we may develop them too. Maybe we choose them for their negative qualities. We want to experience at another's hands the particular qualities and behaviors we feel would either make us dig deep and find resources we did not know we had; or which we know we have ourselves demonstrated previously, and so would like to have a taste of at the receiving end, in order for us to change and grow.

Maybe we choose them for the experiences they have agreed to give us, prior to incarnating. That might be abandonment, loss and bereavement, coldness, being highly critical, whatever. Essentially, we know what experiences will help us grow in certain ways, and the souls who will become our parents agree to give us those. In love and in the service of expansion. Maybe there are lessons that we have agreed, again prior to incarnating, to help our parents to learn. That is, we agree to be the teacher, the giver of the experience, rather than being the receiver. We come, therefore, to teach them what they wish to learn. That includes, at times, coming willingly to suffer certain experiences at their hands in order to lay the foundations of the growth they will benefit from later in life as the consequences and aftermaths unfold.

Whichever the reason may be, whatever the loving contract, it has always been chosen, and we have always bought into it. We knew what we were doing, and we wanted wholeheartedly to do it. And a necessary component for our being able to benefit fully from these choices is that we must forget that we made them. It must be for real. We must not remember that it is only a game. Once we start to think in these terms, understanding, taking responsibility, and letting go, become far more straightforward.

We can allow our higher self to approach our parents' higher selves (or the higher self of whoever we are focusing on), and, in meditation, ask about the decisions we all made prior to incarnation, and why we made those particular choices. What was the purpose, what were the lessons, experiences, unfolding patterns, we were all meant to achieve? And have we achieved what they set out to achieve? If not, what work is there left that we might need still to do? It is very different. We are no longer casting ourselves as helpless victims, but rather we are understanding that we are/were willing and co-operative players, co-operative components, in a purposeful, meaningful, and entirely planned experience.

It is the ability to look at this much bigger picture - essentially of a loving and expanding universe, experiencing itself in and through us - and our place in that bigger picture, that can bring genuine and lasting relief and release.

We might even find it in our hearts to feel appreciation for sacrifices made in love.

We are all that is

You are all that is
and I am all that is
and he is all that is
and so is she
and so are they
and that is all that is
and this is all there is.
There is all of this
and all of that,
and it is all,
all that is.
All of it.
And that is all there is
to say about all of that.
It all simply is.
Simple as that.

Signs

· ·

A chance conversation the other day made me stop and focus. As always, there was something important that it was reminding me to remember. It was that the universe is always giving us signs, if only we notice.

The conversation was with a woman – let us call her Laura - who is always, endlessly, putting others first. To the point of exhaustion. Laura carries a dream inside her that, one day, she will start her own business. She knows it would take off and be very successful, because people ask her to do exactly what she will be offering within that business all the time. She always says to me that she does it because she knows people cannot do it for themselves. Laura says it costs her a great deal in time, and that it does not leave time for other things in her life that she quite like to do, but that she 'feels she ought to do this, because she can.' She possesses a wealth of expertise and experience that few others can offer, and so she shares that as a favor to anyone who asks her, all the time.

She was telling me how someone in the office at work, whom she didn't particularly know, had asked her help in filling out the form which would get her elderly relative the extra funding she needed - this is what she will offer as her expertise when she starts her own business. She agreed to do this willingly, and spent quite a few hours on it. She even delivered it to the woman's home. The work, had she charged for her time, would have cost £350. The woman was delighted. She spent quite some time asking further questions, about other funding she might be able to get. Then she presented the woman who had helped her with a box of chocolates as a thank you. The price on the box, which she had not removed, was £1. I know it is not about the money, but bear with me. The woman also asked if she would do the same for her friend, someone the woman we are talking about did not know at all.

So here is the thing. When she came out of the house of the woman she had been helping, she found a parking ticket on the windscreen of her car.

Something suddenly fell into place, and she discovered that she was extremely angry. Very, very angry. She suddenly saw things in a different light. She realized that the universe was giving her a message. Permission, really, stark and clear. There in the plastic envelope on her car windscreen. It was costing too much. It was costing *her* too much. The cost was too great. And she understood the symbolic message; she got it. It was not about the parking fine. That was not what she was having to pay. She was paying with her leisure time, her love life, her hobbies, her business dream; she was giving *too much*.

It was not that she was suddenly going to turn into a selfish self-seeker who has no time or concern for anyone else. She could never ever be that, she possesses a great deal of kindness and compassion and human warmth. And it was not that she would never help anyone again without charging for it, if the circumstances were such that she felt she wanted to. But 'wanted to' rather than 'ought to because she could.' It was that she was going to start weighing up the cost. Properly. She was going to decide that she mattered too.

And she thanked the universe for the wonderful and timely validation of that truth.

She paid the parking fine full of appreciation for the wakeup call it represented. And she knew just how big that message was, how much it actually contained. She felt tearful and loved and joyful and at peace. She knew the universe loved her, but also that she loved herself. And that same day, she set up her new business.

Can you hear?

Can you hear it?
The Universe whispering:
Isn't this delicious?
I made all this
with you in mind.
I hope you like it!
Have fun!

The awakening trap

Spiritual awakening - realizing that you are not who you think you are - is one of the most profound and life-changing experiences any of us can have. The moment of seeing through the illusions we have believed, and experiencing the freedom of realizing that separation and separateness are illusions, that we are actually all one, all Source energy having a human experience, is one from which we never look back.

However, there is also a trap in this new armor called awakening. I call it armor because, if we are not mindful of how it can go, the very process of 'spiritual awakening' can become just one more barrier against truly living. Let me try to explain what I mean:

We human beings are extremely good at developing strategies - defenses - to help us to deny, or protect ourselves from, reality in the raw. We do not know we are doing it, but we very quickly and readily start to sift through what we experience and categorize it. We decide what is safe and unsafe, good and bad, and then we focus on the aspects of our reality that fit most comfortably with how we want to experience the world. Then we sweep all the other unwanted perceptions away and out of sight. If we do not find it comfortable, or it does not fit, or if it disturbs our neat reality, out it goes.

It is a psychological con, something which we therapists call 'splitting.' We 'split' reality, in order to simplify it for ourselves and to keep it emotionally comfortable. It is part of the way in which we begin to write the story of our life. We focus on certain bits, and we overlook or forget others. It is the defense that is behind every prejudice, every grudge, and every determinedly 'idealistic' memory we ever hold.

Now do not get me wrong, I am all for ideal. I think it would be great if it actually existed. And I do not have a problem with material or experience we have not yet identified or worked through or made conscious getting in our way and coloring our current reality. That is part of the glorious complexity of living this life, and part of the adventure we are embarked upon, and the way it is meant to be.

What I am talking about here, quite specifically, is the splitting we unknowingly get caught up in once we decide that we are awakening. We start saying things like, 'I am not this body, I am a soul.' Or 'everything is an illusion.' Or 'duality does not exist.' I do get it - I get what we are trying to say. We are excited by this new information; it feels wonderfully freeing, liberating, and joyful. And it is, isn't it! That remembering is just wonderful! It solves so many problems. Every problem.... And there you have the bit that is dodgy. There you have the split. There you have the defense.

We can turn into the worst kind of smug spiritual extremist, with quotes and well-known sayings forced down the throats of anyone who asks for help or advice. No matter whether or not they are ready or able or even wanting to hear it; no matter where they happen to be on their own spiritual journey. Even if their path does not happen to coincide with ours. We start to believe there is only one way, and that the only way is our way. We have all come across it; we all know what I mean. When that happens, we have ceased to live responsively to life, to flow easily with the emotional ups and downs of this time/place reality. We have employed yet another defense, one that is pretty frightening: in the process of becoming 'enlightened', we have actually switched off from the Love which is who we are, and instead have ceased to allow that love to flow and become numb. We have ceased to live from the heart, and have taken up a position in our head.

You see, I reckon that spirituality is not about protecting ourselves from the realities of the world and of living this life. It is not about splitting off all the bits we would rather not look at too closely, or feel fully. We do not need to armor ourselves against life, because we are life. The experiencer and the observer, the creator and the creation of it all. It is really very simple. So simple, in fact, that we can easily miss just how simple it is. Spiritual awakening, as I see it, is the ongoing and timeless recognition of who we really are. It is constant and endless. We never reach the conclusion. The day we think we have it all wrapped up is the day we have lost sight of our purpose.

We are consciousness, awareness, pure, loving creative intelligent light energy prior to form, taking form in order to experience and witness physicality and what it is to be human. That is who we are, and why we came. When we truly get that, once we realize and accept and allow that this is who we really are, our defenses become unnecessary. We become the awareness that is living this life, with curiosity and compassion, by choice, to experience all of it, as All That Is. And we embrace this life wholeheartedly.

That is where the real adventure begins. We open our arms and our heart wide and we say yes to the life we have created. All of it, even the bits that do not fit neatly and tidily. Not just when it is going well, but when it is not. We simply embrace our own creation, knowing that this is what it is, with curiosity and wonder, and say *Wow!*

Welcome to ordinary life lived extraordinarily well!

See

See
with different eyes.
Look
into the space
between things.
Notice
what connects us
in the space
between everything.
See
with different eyes.
Look and see.

On who we really are

· ·

It happens all the time in my therapy room. We human beings, eternally evolving souls suffering from temporary amnesia don't seem to be able to resist it. We cause ourselves so much suffering, always, from the way in which we insist on identifying with everything we feel and experience *as if* this is who we actually are. Instead of realizing that we are the observer of what we are feeling and experiencing, the one who watches, we decide that we are the thing we are experiencing.

So, we decide that we are an angry person, when actually we are simply experiencing and observing what it is like to be angry. We decide that we are a jealous person, instead of appreciating that we are simply experiencing and observing the feeling of being jealous. Do you see how different this is? Let us take the example of the sense of badness that troubles so many of us..........

We cannot actually *be* a bad person, we can only experience and feel the feelings of being bad. We cannot actually *be* a feeling; we can only experience and observe the feeling. Or, more accurately still, we can only observe the experiencing of the feeling. That is, we can feel what it is to feel like we are a bad person, but we cannot be a bad person. There is no such thing as a bad human being; there is only a human being experiencing the feeling of being bad.

Feelings come and go; they appear and disappear in us. They are never ever permanent, never fixed. We never *are* this feeling or this reaction. And this feeling or reaction is only ever the tiniest part of everything we are actually feeling. It is simply the bit we are choosing to focus on, just now, in any given moment. We are feeling many other things too, all at the same time. We are simply not choosing to give them our attention. All feelings - any feeling that a human being is capable of feeling - are available for us to experience. All of human experience, all of human consciousness, the entire human condition, is available to us. We are source energy expanding. Much of this we have experienced before, but never before in quite this unique and individual way.

Everything that has gone before is already available to us, and we are at the leading edge of all that is now expanding All That Is further still. It never stops and it is never done, never will be done. Can't ever be done. We are the space that holds all this experience; we are not this experience. We are not limited in this way; we are boundless and limitless, and we experience and observe everything without being the thing we are experiencing and observing. It is what we came here to do, and we are doing it extremely well. That is the beauty of this brief human experiment of a life. For experiment is what it is. It is constantly changing. It is complex. Nothing ever stands still. And we are here to fully experience all of it. We are not defined by it; we are rather the awareness *of* it. We never do become it; we simply observe the experience of it in each timeless and eternal moment. We are both the experiment, the experience embodied in the experiment, and the observer of it all. That is all, and it is everything.

So let's free ourselves to do what we came here to do, and to enjoy it just as we intended when we came. Let's stop judging ourselves and each other. We are all One. We grow through shared experience in this physical reality. And out of this physical reality. Everything you can feel, I can feel too. Everything I can think, you can think also. Everything one of us experiences, we all experience. Over and over again, with each new experience, each new thought. Whatever is known by any becomes part of the expanded wisdom of all. That, surely, is expansion. And as pure consciousness experiencing all of humanity, there can be no good or bad. It all simply *is*.

What an amazing realization that is! What a truly thrilling opportunity! This is one glorious journey of discovery and make believe. No more and no less. And we are in the driving seat! Let us make sure we do not miss a single moment of it!

You are the wave

Resist trying
to define yourself
You are not
your feelings
You are not
your experience
You never ever
stand still
You are the wave
but also
the ocean
You are all things
but also no one thing
Never be defined
for you are
constant movement
You are
Love in motion
forever changing
forever growing
You are the wave
but also
the ocean

Trauma

· ·

We tend to think of the word Trauma as referring to an event that has been 'traumatic.' However, this is not strictly accurate. Trauma is not in the event itself; rather, trauma resides in the nervous system. Trauma is the physical manifestation of memory held in the body. That is, it is physiological and energetic, more than it is psychological. We are energetic beings, and so trauma is an energetic response. I hope that the following might help shed light on why we sometimes experience the reactions we do, and suggest some ways to help ease them, both in the moment, and in an ongoing way.

By trauma, I mean anything from sweaty palms and mild palpitations, to gasping for air and fearing we can't breathe, to shaking uncontrollably and feeling like our body is so weak that our legs will give way, to finding ourselves terrifyingly reliving in the moment memories which are long gone but feel like they are happening now. All are part of a primitive reaction initiated by the oldest and deepest structure in our brain, our fear center, the amygdala. It is triggered whenever we feel in danger, physically, emotionally, psychologically. Most of us know it as the 'fight or flight' response. We understand that it involves a rush of adrenaline and cortisol through our blood stream, which is intended to enable us to protect ourselves by running away or staying to fight.

What is *less* well known is what is called the 'freeze' response. It happens when we *cannot* escape. That is, when we are trapped with no way out, either physically because there is no escape route for us, or emotionally because no-one is recognizing or acknowledging our terror or predicament, or psychologically because we have seen or witnessed something which was frightening and is now embedded in our memory. It doesn't have to be as major as you might think, this memory of helplessness. It is less about the magnitude of the external event, and far more about our response to it, during and after. This is the vital missing link. It explains why we experience panic attacks, and later I will go on to say more about how to overcome them in the light of what is actually going on.

Going into 'freeze' is extremely frightening. We are ok if we can fight or take flight, but if we are helpless - for example, a child listening to parents arguing and threatening to leave or hurt each other, someone involved in a hold-up, someone falling and injuring himself or herself so seriously that they cannot move or attract help - it is a different matter. When fight or flight is either impossible, or perceived to be impossible, instead of being able to move we go limp. Our muscles collapse in fear as the body shuts down in a state of overwhelm.

This is the crucial issue: freeze is the last resort, when no other option seems possible. It is not a conscious choice; it is automatic. I have often had to reassure clients of this when they have felt guilty that they did not respond as they would have liked to have done in the face of a seemingly impossible situation from which there appeared to be no escape. In the face of a real or perceived threat from which we believe we cannot escape, several things happen. At one level, we become totally incapable of moving or responding. We are rooted to the spot, rigid, holding our breath, unable to help ourselves. At the same time, all the physiological responses of 'fight or flight' are still going on. So although we are thrown into a state of immobility, or 'shock', our entire system is on full alert, fully charged.

It does not take much imagination to appreciate just how utterly terrifying that is. Paralyzed but wanting to run, heart pounding, unable to breathe, trembling, the sense of time distorted so that it feels like it goes on forever. Children faced with seemingly inescapable situations tend to go straight to freeze and simply shut down. So what causes the storage of trauma in the body? What determines whether we go on to experience trauma after an event, or we do not? Even more crucial still, how do we prevent the buildup of stored traumatic energy in ourselves, and help those we love - especially our little ones - to avoid the response that will leave them vulnerable to experiencing the trauma response over and over again thereafter. And, if we were one of those little ones, how do we break that cycle *now*?

The answer, crucially, lies in what happens during and after the event that has overwhelmed us. The crucial issue is to avoid being traumatized: the excess buildup of fight or flight energy that could not be put to use must be discharged. When something frightening happens, we need to use up the excess buildup of energy. If we do not, it will stay trapped in the physical body, creating the potential symptoms ever after. Panic attacks come into this category. They are a reliving of a sense that we cannot move, cannot breathe, and cannot escape. Because the memory is held in the body, the body reproduces the traumatic symptoms. We therefore become rigid and tense, we hold our breath or breathe very shallowly, we shake and tremble because, just like an infant, we cannot keep ourselves warm.

I use the term 'memory feelings' with clients. I try to help them know that these responses are memory only, bodily memory, the body remembering only, that they are safe now, powerful now, have choice now. I encourage them to breathe *out*, and release all the air they are holding in their lungs which makes it feel like they cannot breathe. I encourage them to discover that they are able to loosen their muscles once they consciously notice how tight and tense they are. That they can relax and that, as they do so, the frightening physiological symptoms start to ease.

Finally, I encourage them to move. To get up, move about; shake their arms, their legs, their shoulders, and their whole body. To help their body remember that they can move, are not trapped or paralyzed as they believe. Even better, to dance. Wildly, freely, guided by their body to find movements the body needs. Preferably to drumming or a powerful beat or strong vibrational music.

It is only when we do not release this energy that we build vulnerability to trauma. And once the blood and the breath and therefore energy are flowing once again, we need the experience of comfort and safety. To be warm, be reminded that we are safe, to feel empowered, powerful, to visualize how we would react next time, another time.

The sense of 'I am safe' is paramount. This is true of we who are adults, and it is even truer for our little ones. It might be helpful to say a little about this sense of safety. What we can do to help ourselves to feel safe, and to know that we are safe. We need to experience this, initially, viscerally, in our body. It is not an intellectual process. We must *feel* it.

It helps to feel the ground beneath our feet, we need warmth, and to settle ourselves in a familiar place or amongst familiar things. Each of us knows what we need, and we should allow our intuition to guide us. Touch is helpful, except where violence has been part of the trauma, in which case we sometimes need to feel safe from further invasion, and to be reassured that we are in completely in control of what happens to us right now. With this exception, it often helps to feel held, to feel another's arms around us, or to be soothe by another's words speaking reassuringly to us, or to have a blanket enfold us. We need to feel surrounded by kindness, and to feel understood. We especially need to be kind and forgiving to ourselves, to allow and not judge any reaction we might have had, but to understand that, in the moment, we could not help it. That is, to normalize the reaction.

Children need to be held tight, soothed, rocked, stroked and caressed, to hear a soothing and confident, but gentle voice. Until the physical symptoms begin to subside, we are not able or ready to begin to process the experience with our mind.

Once we can feel ourselves begin to feel physically safer, we can begin to remind ourselves that whatever happened is over, it ended, it is not happening now, we survived it. Our task is to gradually change our perception from 'I am in danger' to 'I am safe.' That will often involve rediscovering our ability to move, to run, to get up and leave, to dance. Alternatively, if that is not possible for us, then to rediscover our voice. Or to rediscover the ability to focus our mind and our will. Anything that makes us feel powerful again. For, of-course, we *are* powerful, much more powerful than we manage to remember sometimes whilst we are in the grip of fear.

There are some wonderful projects in existence where mothers/fathers and babies who have experienced trauma - for instance, through war - are helped to overcome that trauma by dancing gently and rhythmically as they hold their babies close in their arms, to background drumming and rhythmic sound. Trauma, panic attacks, recurrent memory feelings of helplessness, running scared, none of these need be something that we dread ever again. We can know we are powerful and free. We just have to taste that we can take charge again.

And we can help the little ones in our care to feel the power they truly have, rather than the perceived lack of empowerment which builds the vulnerability that will leave them open to panic attacks and trauma response in their future. Talking about what we might have done, or would do another time, and visualizing our creating a very different outcome, one where we remain powerful and in control, is also enormously helpful. We can also help ourselves to remember that we came here as powerful creators, not as helpless victims. Sometimes, in the throws and aftermath of frightening or challenging experiences, it can be difficult to hold onto this truth, let alone to embrace it. But there is, nevertheless, enormous strength and healing to be gained if we able to do so.

Trauma does not have to be permanent; neither do its effects have to be destructive or debilitating. We begin to heal the moment we start to know that we are safe, and to let go of fear. To find our way back to safety, to know that we are loved, and then to find once again the love that we all are. The moment we can find that reality again, we find relief.

We are, after all, powerful manifesters of our reality; what we believe is what we see, and what we see is what becomes our reality, and this truth never ever changes. It can be no other way.

What a wonderful thought to hold!

Jamie

· ·

Another story…

Are you sitting comfortably? Then I will begin…

Jamie had lived with his grandmother and grandfather for as long as he could remember. He knew he had at one time had a dad, but he had died when he was a few months old. No one spoke about his mum. He learned that neither should he.

Some things about living in this house that he called home were really nice. He liked the fields at the bottom of the garden, which often had cows in them. He liked standing on the bottom rung of the swing gate and holding out clumps of grass in his hand to see if one would dare to come and take it from him. And one often did. He liked watching them swish their tails and thought their long eye lashes were very beautiful.

And his grandfather would always tease him and make him laugh. He had fun playing outside in the garden, and the days when his grandfather would be out in the greenhouse, and would let him help m, plants seedlings or take cuttings, were magical and gave him a sense of how peaceful and easy life could be. Jamie was close to his grandfather.

However, there were other things about living there that did not feel so good. Inside the house, it did not feel as easy or as happy. Jamie always felt anxious in there. There was a way that people were with each other that he did not understand. And it frightened and unsettled him.

So, for instance, Jamie would watch his grandmother having a cup of tea with a neighbor, one of her friends. And they would gossip and laugh - a bit unkindly, Jamie noticed - about everyone else they knew. All the other neighbors in the street, and all their friends. But although Jamie thought some of the things they said were a bit mean, he knew they must be true, because what adults said always was true.

But then it would get more puzzling and confusing. Because the next day, Jamie would see his grandmother having a cup of tea with another neighbor, also a friend. However, here is the thing. Jamie would listen and watch as his grandmother gossiped and laughed with this neighbor, about everyone else in their street, everyone they knew. Including - and this was the thing that left Jamie feeling frightened and worried - the neighbor that she had been so friendly with the day before. And the neighbor she had been having a cup of tea with the day before, had been laughing with her and saying mean things about *this* neighbor that she was being so friendly with today.

Jamie pondered this a lot. And the more he pondered it, the heavier his heart became. He would watch his grandmother being smiley and friendly with anyone who came to the door, or who spoke with her on the telephone, one moment, and then calling them names and mimicking them and sneering at them the next. With a cold feeling of dread all the way along his spine, he began to understand what this world was really like. This adult world. He began to understand that people did not mean what they said. That they would say one thing to your face and another behind your back. That everyone hated everyone else, while just pretending to like them.

He began to notice more and more things that confirmed this. He noticed the way that his grandmother behaved with his grandfather. She would always try to make him feel bad. Sort of guilty. As if he had never got it right, never done enough, was a bit stupid. He noticed, too, that the grandfather that he saw in the house was a different grandfather to the one he loved spending time with outside.

When they were together outside, they laughed and joked and talked about anything and everything. Jamie knew that his grandfather enjoyed their chats and doing things with him. At least, he had thought he knew that. It had always seemed that way. Seemed. Jamie realized that everything seemed, but then was not. It was all just seemed. His grandmother seemed to like people, but did not really. Jamie was trying to get his head around seemed. Maybe his grandfather only seemed to enjoy his company. But didn't really. Would maybe say something horrible about him to his grandmother in secret once he was not there.

The grandfather Jamie saw in the house was subdued, did not say much, and was sort of wary and careful. He did not laugh or tease, in fact he did not pay Jamie much attention at all. If he did, Jamie's grandmother would sniff loudly, or sigh, or bang something down on a surface, or tell his grandfather to do something she needed doing. Like his grandfather was not allowed to pay him any attention. Like it made her upset. Jamie did not fully understand it, but he fully felt it. In addition, he also knew that, inside all the sniffing and the banging and the carrying on, his grandmother carried a deep, deep sadness, and that his grandfather knew that.

And so, gradually, Jamie learned to become careful and wary too. He learned to watch his grandmother and to know what mood she was in, and to adapt the way he was so that she would not sniff or bang things down loudly because of something he had said or done. He learned to anticipate what she might want him to do, and to do it even before he was asked. And bit by bit, he stopped having fun with his grandfather too. Life was a serious business, and a worry.

And Jamie's heart grew heavier and heavier. When he went to school, he did not know how it was that the children there seemed to be able to play. How they could just let themselves run around squealing and shouting like that. He felt the grip of familiar anxiety in his stomach at the thought of what his grandmother would say to him if he were to ever behave that way.

And so Jamie became ever more isolated, ever more different. He was different in so many ways. Not just ordinary, obvious things like he did not have a mum or a dad, that he lived with his grandparents, that he didn't know how to play properly with the other children. But other things too. Like he knew how to watch, and notice. He always knew what was going on inside people; he felt their feelings. And he was gentle, kind. It was as if the cows in the field knew that, too. Animals always sensed it.

His teachers were concerned, and spoke to his grandmother about how he seemed very unhappy. However, as he sat beside his grandmother in the classroom, as she listened to his teacher expressing enormous concern for him, and told his teacher what a contented little boy he always seemed at home, he knew that there was nothing that could be done. When his teacher asked him, in front of his grandmother, if there was anything troubling him, he smiled in that way he knew he was expected to smile, and told her, in that way he knew he was expected to tell her, that everything was fine.

Then, one day, a very strange thing happened. Jamie was sitting down the bottom of the garden, where he had been feeding some grass to the cows in the field beyond, his back against the swing gate, when he heard someone call his name. His first instinct was to look back towards the house, thinking that it was his grandmother calling him to ask him to do something for her, but as he looked, there was no sign of her. Maybe he had imagined it. He often did imagine that he heard her voice. It was always inside his head. But then, there it was again. Definitely his name. And definitely not his grandmother's voice. It was too kindly, and it had too much laughter in it, too much warmth, to be her voice. The sound of a kindly voice actually had a sudden surprising effect on him, and before he realized quickly enough to stop it, he found himself crying.

Jamie never cried. Never ever. His grandmother would have had no patience with it and would have told him he was putting it on. But now he was crying. And once he started, he found that he could not stop.

He sat, hands clasped around his legs, head resting on his knees, for a long time, sobbing and sobbing. He had not known there was so much sobbing inside him. Now it was coming out and he did not seem to be able to put it away. He wondered if he would ever stop.

But gradually, he became aware of something enveloping him. It felt strange, sort of like a buzzy, warm, safe feeling. There were not really words to describe it. It was like having arms around him, only not like ordinary arms. These were bigger, for a start. They wrapped around and covered all of him. Then they seemed to squeeze him tight and, as they did so, he felt an enormous well of something building in him. Sort of both in him and outside of him and all around him. He could not really tell where it was exactly. But it was the most wonderful, soothing, satisfying, deep embrace he had ever known. And for several minutes, he found himself sinking right into it.

And as he did so, he suddenly realized so many things. He understood this feeling because he knew he *remembered* it. It was like coming home. It was such a big remembering that he found himself holding his breath. So, so many things. Then, in the middle of this amazing feeling, a presence. A something. And as he felt this something, he raised his head and looked up. He gasped, because the entire world was shimmering. Sparkling. He had never seen anything so beautiful.

And in the midst of the shimmering, this something that was both outside him, all around him and yet right in the most secret places right inside him. And, as he was trying to take it all in, the strangeness of it, the wonder of it, he suddenly knew something else. On top of all that he had already remembered, he found himself remembering who his grandmother really was. All they had known, all they had been. He remembered the *feeling* of her, the *sense* of her. Not the grandmother who gossiped and sneered and bullied. Not her. No, this was the grandmother who had been many things to him, and who he loved. Who loved him. He remembered.

Suddenly, he jumped up. He wanted to run to her, to see if she remembered too. He was sure she would. He knew she would. He went racing in through the back door, calling for her. He was no longer worried that she would shout at him for forgetting to take his boots off first.

But as he ran into the kitchen, he was met by the sight of his grandfather kneeling beside a chair, holding his grandmother's hand, head laid in her lap, crying softly. He did not quite understand at first. She seemed to be very still.

His grandfather did not notice him standing there for a while. Jamie stood quietly, taking it all in. Something had happened to his grandmother, clearly. Otherwise, his grandfather would not be so upset. But now, his grandfather had become noticeably calm, still, peaceful. He seemed to be concentrating. Like he was listening. He was not crying anymore. He was somewhere else.

Then, suddenly, Jamie felt the hug again. He did not know what else to call it. The hug that seemed to come from inside him and outside of him and everywhere else all at the same time. It was even stronger than before, and seemed to be somehow linked to the woman who was his grandmother but was now very still.

And then something else happened. For the rest of his life he never could quite explain to anyone how it was that he heard what he heard. Nothing was said aloud, and it was not really words. Whenever he would talk about it in the future, he would say it was a sort of knowing. That he felt and knew, rather than heard, what was being conveyed. It was as if he was hearing it from every possible place at once. Like the whole universe was communicating with him. But at the same time he knew it was his grandmother. It was very definitely his grandmother.

And what he felt, or heard, with a knowing in his whole being was this:

'This is for you, Jamie. For you and for the rest of your time here on earth: Be happy. Be amazing. Be all you came here to be. Be all I came here to help you to be. And never forget you are so loved. So loved. Always and in every way. You have such great things ahead of you, my precious one. It's going to be incredible.'

And it was!

You are not random

You are not random.
You were never random,
never could be.
How could it ever be
that you,
the universe made visible,
with gifts that only you can bring,
and secrets only you can tell,
and experience which only you can offer,
in your own unique and never to be repeated way,
and with wisdom which only you possess,
and qualities which are yours alone,
and knowing all you will go through
on behalf of all of us,
joys, fears, challenges, growing and being,
could ever be thought to be random?
You are a child of the universe,
purposeful, powerful, limitless,
here because you chose to be here.
You are filled with the wisdom of the ages,
and surrounded by the Love
of All That Is.
You have too much tender guidance,
and more willing help,
too many eyes watching and more arms embracing,
too much magic and miracles at your fingertips,
way too much loving energy

pulsing and radiating
in and around and through and from you
for you to ever be random.
To think that you are random,
in the face of all this which you are,
and have been, and will be,
is so random as to be simply ridiculous.
Random!? You!?
How random is that!

You are exactly where you need to be

You are exactly where you need to be. There are no accidents, none of this is random. You are creating this experience that is all about you *for you.*

So who are *you?* What are *you?*

Supposing there is not really a *you,* in quite the way you might think about it at all. Supposing that, in any given moment, you were simply Awareness, or Essence, experiencing what it is like to *be* you? That you are so much more than you ever allowed yourself to imagine? What if it is not so much that you are living this life, but that life is flowing *through* you, and that you *are* that life?

Supposing that you are pure Essence, Life Force, flowing in the flow? Along with *all* of us? In Oneness? One magnificent forever-expanding energy, light energy, All That Is, pure Source energy, that has no beginning and no end, has always been and always will be? Would that leave you feeling bereft, or might you find it wonderfully liberating? That there is no 'Other' out there, simply a single, complex, evolving and expanding, beautiful energy of light and love, of which you are a vital part? That you are both a drop in the ocean but, also, the ocean itself.

I believe that we are, indeed, Essence or Awareness. I believe that we have chosen to manifest as this pure essence many times, and journeyed many lifetimes. That this has been in different cultures, different regions, different times, and as different genders. And that we have done so, every single time, along with other tender souls who belong to our Soul Family. I believe that, with them, we have shared joys and sorrows, hardship, suffering and abundance, and everything in between. And I know that the reason that I recognize members of my soul family, every single time we encounter each other, is not because they look the same, or sound the same, or even behave the same. It is because I recognize their energy – their Essence – just as they recognize mine.

I believe that every choice you ever made is exactly the choice you needed to make at the time for you to evolve. And that this is true for me, also. And for all of us. And I believe that every single 'mistake' you ever chose to make was exactly the mistake you needed to make at the time for you to evolve. And that this true of me, also. And of all of us. If you can allow and not resist this fundamental truth, you will find peace. You will feel known as you have never before felt known, with a knowing which has existed down all the ages. And you will feel loved as you have never before felt loved, with a tenderness and compassion, an unconditional acceptance and joyful celebration of all you are, and a deep appreciation for all you have been willing to go through in the service of expansion of All That Is. You will know and feel how intrinsically you belong to the Oneness of all things, and as such are loved and cherished and supported beyond measure.

Feel the depth and power of this. Take it in. Feel the power of it, the freedom of it, the responsibility and sacred trust of it. The fun of it and the daring, playful adventure in it.

Then relax, let go, and enjoy the ride!

A pair of old magic spectacles

· ·

I have an old pair of spectacles.
Magic spectacles.
When I put them on,
something happens
to my eyes,
or, more accurately, to my vision.
What I see changes.
These old spectacles
came to me
a very long time ago.
I can hear the voices
of all who have worn them
before me,
just as those who come after me
will hear my voice, too.
We are the old ones,
the wise ones,
the spinners and the weavers of the web,
the teachers and the healers,
the many voices
become the one voice.
For I am you, just as you are me,
and together we all share the one heart.
We are magnificent and beautiful beyond imagining,
and love and compassion beyond measure.
We are the dancers among the stars.................